WORLD SOURDOUGHS
FROM ANTIQUITY

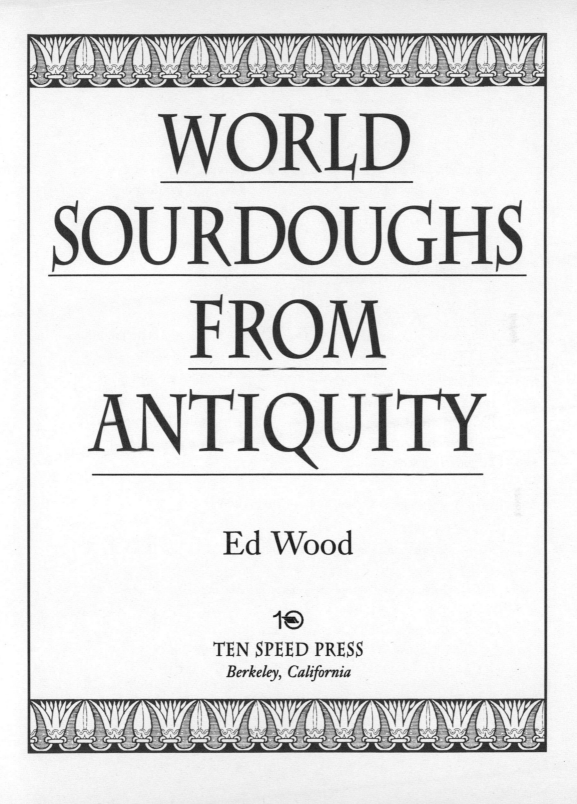

WORLD SOURDOUGHS FROM ANTIQUITY

Ed Wood

TEN SPEED PRESS
Berkeley, California

1☉

Ten Speed Press
Box 7123
Berkeley, California 74707

Distributed in Australia by E. J. Dwyer Pty. Ltd., in Canada by Publishers Group West, in New Zealand by Tandem Press, in South Africa by Real Books, and in the United Kingdom and Europe by Airlift Books.

Cover and text design by Nancy Austin
Photographs of statue on front cover and grains on back cover © 1993 by Kenneth Garrett. Photograph of bread on front cover by Judith Vevjoda and Scott Vlaun.

Library of Congress Cataloguing-in-Publication Data

Wood, Ed, 1926-
     World sourdoughs from antiquity / Ed Wood. — [Rev. ed.]
       p. cm.
     Includes bibliographical references and index.
     ISBN 0-89815-843-5
     1. Cookery (Sourdough) 2. Bread. I. Title.
  TX770.S66W66   1996   96-28621
  641.8'15—dc20   CIP

Printed in Canada
First printing, 1996
1 2 3 4 5 6 7 8 9 10 — 00 99 98 97 96

 CONTENTS

 Acknowledgments

Many people, from the deserts of Saudi Arabia to the lush valleys and mountains of Idaho, participated in baking and tasting the recipes in this book. Their comments and suggestions have improved and enhanced the material herein.

Our Egyptian adventure, described in Chapter 1, would not have been possible without the support of numerous friends and colleagues. To name a few, Tom Donndelinger, M.D., introduced me to Charlie Smith, M.D., a radiotherapist at the Mountain States Tumor Institute who supervised the radiation exposure under the capable hands of Doug Hughes, RT, that produced the sterile flour essential to our reproduction of ancient Egyptian baking methods. Lorenz Shaller of KUSA did the impossible by finding 50 pounds of emmer for us to take back to its home in Egypt. And then there is Mark Lehner, Ph.D., who discovered the ancient bakery at Giza and convinced the National Geographic Society to support the baking project. Ellie Rogers, Ken Garrett, Chris Sloan, and David Roberts rounded out the team that built the Egyptian bakery and provided the moral support to keep us going. The faculty of the Department of Plant Sciences at North Dakota State University supplied invaluable information on new varieties of durum with improved gluten.

One person in Idaho stands out as student, critic, and then teacher. Bob Linville of New Meadows, Idaho, has taught me as much as I have taught him. My apologies for not being able to name the many other individuals who have urged us to complete this book and bring sourdoughs back to life.

Thanks also goes to my wife, Jean, who did the original proofing and editing and the complete electronic production of the manuscript.

PREFACE

THE MAGIC OF SOURDOUGHS CAPTURED my imagination over fifty years ago and has entranced me to this day. Over the years, I have marveled at the charisma of the wild yeast that leavened humankind's first bread and fed the world for almost five thousand years. Unfortunately, the art and technique of making sourdoughs is disappearing from our culture. I wrote this book to prevent that. This is a no-nonsense book for those who are serious about sourdoughs. It doesn't reveal shortcuts or easy ways to bake what the world remembers as sourdough because there are none.

The curse of sourdough bread is commercial yeast—in particular, instant dried yeast. Sourdough flavor is produced by a fermentation process that requires 12 to 24 hours, and commercial yeasts grow so fast that the fermentation is never completed, if it gets started at all. Yet for the past fifty years sourdough "experts" have advocated using commercial yeast not only to leaven sourdoughs but to form the initial sourdough culture. Small wonder that the sourdoughs of history have almost disappeared.

Over the last century monumental things have happened to bread making. The industrial revolution took it out of the home and put it in factories that manufactured something labeled "bread." The same revolution took us out of the home, too, and in many ways we have become as hurried as today's bread. But the faster we run, the more we look back. Perhaps that explains the rebirth of sourdoughs. Today, as I write this on my computer with a snow-swept Idaho mountain in view, the buzzword is the information highway. The fax across the room hums as an order for one of my sourdough cultures slides into the receiving tray. A glance confirms that it has come from information on the Internet. And I am warmed by the evidence that others out there are searching for real sourdoughs.

1

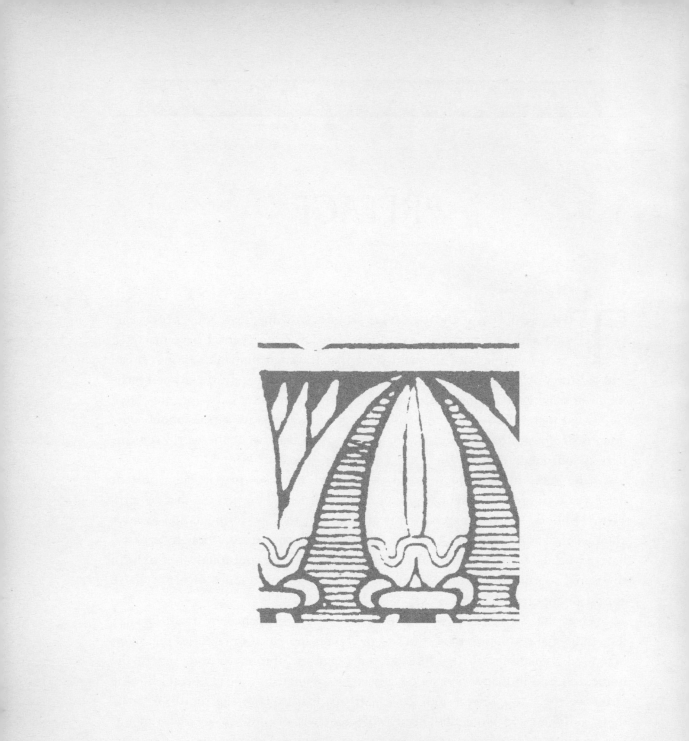

INTRODUCTION

A TRUE SOURDOUGH IS NOTHING MORE than flour and water with wild yeast to make it rise and special bacteria to provide the flavor. Before commercial yeast, all bread was made from sourdough. Every baker, every household, had a wild sourdough culture with special and often secret recipes. For nearly five thousand years, it was thought that something divine created the bubbles in dough and made the loaves grow bigger and bigger. Only one essential factor was clearly recognized: from each batch of dough a sample had to be saved and passed on to the next batch, or the divine "thing" was lost. Sourdough is a living remnant of ancient history that has survived for more than fifty centuries and is as alive today as it was in 3000 B.C.

With the advent of commercial yeast in the late 1800s, the art of bread making gradually changed. In the last fifty years, pressed cake yeast and instant dried yeast have almost totally replaced the use of wild sourdoughs. In the process the intrinsic flavor has been lost. The natural process of rising and fermentation of sourdough requires about 24 hours—far too long for large-volume bakeries. As a result, most sourdough available in the marketplace has been produced by fast-acting commercial yeast spiked with a variety of artificial flavoring agents and chemicals to produce bread that has a sour taste but little resemblance to the flavor of sourdoughs of the past.

Recently, however, several factors have resulted in a resurgence of *authentic* sourdough methods. Foremost is the innate satisfaction in nurturing a sourdough culture from its resting stage into a vigorous, living, pushing, vibrant force that produces something new and special and yet as old as mankind. A loaf of hot sourdough exudes an aroma with an overpowering, irresistible attraction that can be experienced only in the warmth of one's own kitchen. It cannot be purchased anywhere. No other bread is anything like it. If there is an endorphin in the kitchen, it is in the divine "thing" that makes bread rise!

I am frequently asked if different sourdough cultures produce breads that are different. In various tastings of breads made using the Middle Eastern and European sourdoughs we have collected, the participants always find that the breads differ in flavor, sourness, and texture. Small wonder, since there are hundreds, probably thousands, of yeast and bacteria combinations in different sourdoughs that determine the end product. Some rise rapidly, some slowly. Some are delicious, some awful. The combinations that survive for extended periods develop a symbiotic relationship between the yeast and bacteria; that is, each provides something essential to the other. It has been shown, for example, that some yeasts do not use certain carbohydrates found in flour that are required by their bacterial partners. The bacteria, in return, produce antibiotics that protect both the yeast and the bacteria themselves from destruction by other organisms.

Authentic sourdough requires wild yeast. A sourdough baker *never* adds anything to the sourdough culture but flour and water and never uses commercial yeast in any form. Yet many cookbooks give directions for using dry yeast in "sourdough" recipes and even for starting sourdough cultures.

This book flavors sourdoughs with a bit of science, counters years of fiction with grains of fact, and most of all, brings *real* sourdough back to life. It tells the history of sourdough and describes how and where I found sourdough cultures reaching back to the first breads of civilization.

There are three grains in the ingredients chapter that will make you fall in love with sourdoughs, if nothing else does. Two of them have been used for more than five thousand years in baking sourdoughs. Kamut apparently originated in the Middle East, although what it is and where it really came from are shrouded in controversy. Spelt has been used for baking gourmet breads in Europe for centuries, some say for more than nine thousand years. Both of these grains are now grown organically in this country, and the flours from them produce sensational sourdough breads. The third grain, durum wheat, has never been used in bread, but new strains developed in North Dakota will soon change that. Durum is the wheat used in pastas. Try it with sourdoughs and discover something really new!

The last ten years have seen some remarkable changes for the home baker, not the least of which is the bread machine. Can a sourdough purist relate to a bread machine? Probably not. But a lot of folks have rediscovered the pleasures and aroma of hot, fresh bread in their own kitchens by using them. That alone warrants a chapter on the subject. Sourdoughs can be baked successfully in bread machines, but doing so usually takes more than pushing a button and walking away.

Shortly after I published the first edition of *World Sourdoughs from Antiquity*, I met Tanya Bevin, a Russian tour guide who has resided in the Puget Sound area of Washington state for the past twenty or so years. Tanya had written in a letter that her biggest culture shock in coming to the United States was the bread and that she hoped sourdoughs would be different. I had just acquired a sourdough from Finland, and I sent her a sample of the fresh moist culture. In return, on a subsequent trip to Russia, she brought us two Russian cultures, and our lives have never been the same. The Russian culture is surprisingly active and well suited for use in bread machines.

CHAPTER 1

BACK TO THE FIRST SOURDOUGH

IN THE FALL OF 1991 I WAS IDLY reading a day-old edition of the *Idaho Statesman* when I was transfixed by an obscure item buried on an inner page. An archaeologist had just reported the excavation of a large, ancient bakery near the pyramids of Giza. The story of Dr. Mark Lehner's discovery suggested just one thing to me—an opportunity to isolate a sourdough culture that leavened man's first bread from the walls of that bakery. I picked up the telephone and called the Oriental Studies Institute at the University of Chicago and asked for Dr. Lehner. He was still in Egypt. A little cajoling produced a Cairo phone number where he might be reached if one were really lucky or persistent. The time difference was nine hours, but I dialed at once. The gods smiled and Mark Lehner answered the phone. He was eager to reproduce the techniques used by early Egyptians, but knew virtually nothing about baking and perhaps less about the wild yeasts in sourdoughs. We agreed I could help in this area.

It was just before Christmas in that same year when I spoke again with Mark Lehner. He had recently returned to Chicago from the excavation site of the ancient bakery. It had been built in 2500 B.C. to feed the thousands of workers who built the pyramids at Giza. He knew archaeology, but he did not know sourdough baking and needed help. I thought we could probably capture a wild yeast in Giza—possibly progeny from the same organisms that had leavened bread for the pyramid builders. And I knew how to do it. But the weeks stretched into months without another word.

Then, in early March 1993, the phone rang, and Ellie Rogers, an illustrations editor with the *National Geographic* magazine, asked if I would like to help

Lehner and a team from the magazine rediscover how the Egyptians baked the first leavened bread. Would I ever! The team was meeting with the editor the very next day in Washington, D.C., to present the project, and I was invited to join them. I scrambled.

Before the meeting started, I met David Roberts, the writer selected for the project. Roberts was no stranger to the *National Geographic*, but on that day he was nervous. The meeting with editor Bill Graves, which Roberts expected would last for no more than 10 minutes, would determine whether or not we would do the feature. In Roberts's opinion, it could go either way. We hustled over to the National Geographic office, where I met Ellie Rogers; Ken Garrett, the project's photographer; and Chris Sloan, a staff artist. Mark Lehner was the only team member missing. Shortly before the meeting was scheduled, a big guy popped into the room. His name didn't register, but we exchanged small talk about the bread project for perhaps two minutes. Then he turned to go and, with a nod in my direction, said, "I think we should support this." After he was gone, I said, "I like that guy's attitude. Who is he?" Rogers winced and told me, "That was Bill Graves and he just approved your baking project!"

The plan was to leave in mid-April of 1993 and to spend three to four weeks in the Giza area. There was some doubt as to whether Egyptian authorities would permit us to actually conduct our experiments in the ancient bakery that Lehner had discovered or even to have access to the baking vessels and tools that he had recovered. In fact, the bakery had been covered with sand to protect it from the elements. As an alternative, Lehner had proposed that we build a replica somewhere in the desert near the pyramids and have the baking dishes and molds reproduced by a local pottery maker. The highest priority would be to reproduce the actual methods the Egyptians used to produce the leavened bread that fed the pyramid builders.

It's a little difficult to convince anyone you're serious about reproducing an ancient Egyptian bread if you're planning to use refined white, bleached flour. We were serious. The original breads were flatbreads made from barley, which has no gluten. Gluten, the protein that gives wheat flour its cohesiveness and elasticity, is an absolute prerequisite for leavening. At some point the flatbreads seen in tomb drawings began to be replaced by leavened breads of various shapes, meaning that the Egyptians had begun to use the ancestors of modern wheat. All of the wheats belong to the genus *Triticum* and evolved from various wild grasses. One of the first wheats to develop was emmer, *T. dicoccum*. As I left D.C., the only place I knew of to start looking for emmer was Turkey, where a few fields of the ancient grain were still in production.

Safely back on my Idaho mountain, I started the search for emmer. I knew when I made my first call and had to spell "emmer," it wasn't going to be easy. I sensed that I was getting closer when someone pointed me to Lorenz Schaller. He is the founder of the KUSA Society, which maintains a collection of thousands of seeds from around the world and champions the view that natural grains are substances of value that are rapidly disappearing. "KUSA" is a transliterated Sanskrit word meaning "sacred grass." Schaller could spell emmer. He was intrigued by the Egyptian project and immediately offered his resources. Four weeks later, 50 pounds of emmer were delivered to my door, and I milled it into flour.

I felt we needed a backup flour in case the emmer didn't perform as expected. It had to be something that had been grown in Egypt, and the only other grain I knew of was Kamut, classified as *Triticum polonicum*, and it was readily available from a Montana farmer. Kamut is closely related to emmer but is considerably more recent on the evolutionary chain. It is a naked wheat, meaning that the husks literally fall off during threshing. The husks of emmer cling tightly to the grain and are difficult to remove, and so when the naked wheats appeared they quickly replaced emmer.

Once I had secured the emmer and Kamut, I needed to find a way to sterilize the flours to kill any microorganisms that might be present. I wanted the Egyptian sourdough to contain wild yeasts captured in Giza, not ones imported from the United States. Dry heat at the high temperatures needed for sterilization would damage the gluten and render the flour unsuitable for baking. Ultraviolet light might be satisfactory, but there was no data on its application to flour and no equipment available in the area. Ionizing radiation seemed a possibility, but calls to numerous sources indicated that no one had used it for that purpose. I turned to Tom Donndelinger, M.D., pathologist at the Mercy Medical Center in Nampa, Idaho. Donndelinger is an innovator with a talent for recruiting people with specialized expertise. He took my call with the same enthusiasm demonstrated by everyone at the mention of the project in Egypt. "I'll get back to you," he promised, and two hours later he did. He had contacted Charlie Smith, M.D., a therapeutic radiologist at the Nampa offices of the Mountain States Tumor Institute and explained the problem. Smith thought his equipment could sterilize just about anything, but he didn't know any more about irradiating flour than I did.

We set up an experimental protocol using quart Mason jars filled with Kamut.

The jars were exposed to three cesium radiation sources in a chamber used to eliminate certain types of cells from blood. We elected to try 50,000, 100,000, and 150,000 rads for the first series. That's a lot of radiation, and we were pretty sure that something in that range would do the job. But just to be sure, the laboratory at Mercy would run microbiology tests to see if anything had survived.

After the first series, I did bake tests to evaluate the condition of the gluten. It was excellent. The microbiological tests required several days, and I was on pins and needles waiting for the results. When they came, I couldn't believe it. None of them were sterile! So the next series was run at 500,000, 1,000,000, and 1,500,000 rads. Those exposures took approximately 12 hours to complete and only one jar could be exposed at a time. When the jars came out of the irradiation chamber, the two highest exposures had actually changed the color of the glass. The jar that had been exposed to 1.5 million rads was a dark brown color, and we were concerned that it might also be quite brittle. All three samples were sterile, however, and more bake tests showed that the gluten was completely undamaged. With a dosage of 500,000 rads established, we irradiated the rest of the flour I would need for the Egyptian project.

My wife and I had our passports renewed, and we sent them to Ellie Rogers, who had promised to hand-carry them to the Egyptian consulate for our April visas. Then disaster struck—we learned that the Egyptian trip had been canceled! We never found out what actually happened, but the end result was the temporary replacement of the director of the Egyptian Antiquities Society. His successor was not allowing any foreign archaeological expeditions until the heat was off, whatever that meant.

Rogers called to discuss the situation. Long experience had made him philosophical about Middle Eastern politics, and he predicted that the cancellation was only temporary. There was nothing to do, he said, but put everything on the back burner.

During the summer months we took every opportunity to complete the myriad small details, so we would be ready if the call came. It didn't. We had all sorts of baking equipment packed and ready to go. The Tumor Institute irradiated additional Kamut and some white bread flour. I called Rogers and convinced him that we would need a thermocouple to measure the temperature in the ancient ovens we would be using. This gadget consists of a long wire probe connected to a digital readout that would record temperatures where we couldn't see a conventional thermometer. Still no call. We checked and rechecked everything on our lists. By mid-August I was planning an elk hunt for September. The last person I wanted to hear from was Ellie Rogers. That did it. The phone rang, and he asked, "Can you be ready by September 8th?"

After arriving in Washington, we learned that there would be another delay. The Egyptian consulate had told Rogers that they could not guarantee access to many of the areas that were essential to the success of the project. He worked to resolve the problem, and the National Geographic travel department made and changed reservations hourly. Finally, after a week of anxious waiting, we were on our way to Cairo. At last I met the Egyptologist who started it all. I knew at first glance that Mark Lehner was one of those likable characters who could take it and dish it out. Over the ensuing weeks we did plenty of both.

Our first challenge came at Egyptian customs. I had several large packing boxes crammed with our baking utensils and flours; I was particularly concerned about the latter. Getting food materials across country boundaries can be difficult. In preparation, we had contacted an official at the Egyptian Agricultural Research Center, who promised to meet us at customs and clear the way. "No problem," he promised. He never showed. Fortunately, Ken Garrett, with his enormous supply of photographic equipment, captured their total attention. By the time they had inspected and cataloged his every lens and camera body, they simply waved my boxes through.

The next stop was Mena House Oberoi. First built as a royal hunting lodge in the mid-1800s, it was converted to a guest facility for the festivities associated with the opening of the Suez Canal in 1869. It is one of the most beautiful and popular hotels of the Middle East, with some of its decor dating back to the fourteenth century. It is built on a hillside and seems to emanate directly from the base of the Great Pyramid of Khufu.

My first priority was to capture Giza's wild yeasts. I started at once. The balcony of our ground-floor location gave ready access to cats and other creatures. However, Ken Garrett's upper-level room looked ideal. His balcony extended virtually into the center of a giant date palm. Huge, succulent clumps of ripening dates oozed juices and odors that wafted by on the hot, incoming breezes. I have never seen a more fertile or lush environment. In the immediate background, almost close enough to touch, stood the Giant Pyramid. It was perfect. The plan was to expose a mixture of sterile white bread flour and water to the elements for as long as necessary. I didn't think it would take long. On the second day the first bubbles appeared, and on the third the mixture was well on the way to becoming a first-rate active culture.

While I was working with the culture and acquiring other baking supplies in Cairo, the others were searching for an appropriate place to build the bakery replica. When they found a possible site, they'd call us for approval. We rejected one locality after another until the team found an Egyptian Shangri-la nestled in an isolated spot in the agricultural belt not far from the Nile, with the pyramid of Sakkara in the background. Construction began forthwith.

Lehner's ancient bakery consisted of multiple outdoor units capable of producing enough bread to feed an estimated 30,000 people per day. Our objective was to reproduce just one of those units, which was about 20 feet square, with low stone walls approximately 30 inches high. The inner working space was about 10 feet wide. Small indentations in the floor of the original units were probably made by poles and indicated an overhead canopy to provide some protection from the sun. In the floor along one wall was a double row of some fifteen larger indentations, which Lehner believed were for bread molds. This area was deep in charcoal dust, the apparent fuel for baking.

The bread molds represented a major challenge. Compared to modern bread pans, these things were huge. Roughly the shape of a monstrous football, the molds were constructed in two cone-shaped pieces. The larger molds, when put together, were at least 30 inches in length and some 18 inches in diameter at the middle where the two halves meet. Chris Sloan produced a clay model from photographs Lehner had taken in the ancient bakery, and we made a trip to the Belly of the Cow.

The Belly of the Cow! Dante's Inferno would be a more apt term. Acre after acre of huge kilns spew smoke and ash into the environment day and night, month after month. Most of Cairo's pottery is produced here. The fuel is largely garbage, of which there is no shortage. The filth is beyond description. We made our way to the partially underground establishment of a potter and used Sloan's model to negotiate our requirements. The potter initially balked at our schedule, insisting that it would take much longer than we had expected, which would have seriously threatened the schedules of several team members. But compromises were made and a deal was struck. The bread molds would be ready in a little over a week.

One late afternoon we made a trip to the tomb of Teti, located just south of Sakkara, the city of the dead. The entrance to the area wasn't more than a 5-minute drive from our bakery site, and Lehner wanted the team to see the wall drawings depicting Egyptian customs. These drawings were beautifully done, with great detail of ancient Egyptian life. Everything pertaining to offerings for the departed Pharaoh, from the slaughtering of cattle to bread making, was depicted from floor to ceiling. Among the offerings were great loaves of cone-shaped bread, one balanced on each shoulder of a human figure. The bases of the cones rest on the shoulder, with the tips projecting upward. They are, in fact, the exact shape of half of a bread mold. Some Egyptologists had theorized that the dough would rise to fill both halves of the mold and that the bakers would simply cut the finished loaves in half. On the walls of the tomb we saw Egyptians kneading bread, pouring dough into pots, removing bread, and stacking pots over a bed of charcoal. Stacking pots? Where did that fit in? Some archaeologists thought that these drawings showed the pots being fired after the potter has formed them. Others thought that the molds were being heated before the dough was placed in them. As it turned out, those drawings depicted a crucial part of the process, although we didn't know it at the time.

While the pottery was being made and the bakery was being constructed, we set out to find several ingredients and supplies that we would need for baking. Chief among these were charcoal, white flour, barley flour, and some type of lard or oil to apply to the bread molds to keep the bread from sticking. All were available in Egypt five thousand years ago. Our Egyptian driver could barely communicate in English, and we had more than a little trouble in making our needs known. "Charcoal," for example, caused a lot of head shaking before we discovered that their English term for it is "black wood." We used a lot of black wood before the project was finished. It came from Giza's poorest neighborhoods and apparently represented a major source of income to the households supplying it. As it was in ancient times, wood is scarce in modern Egypt and has to be brought in from some distance. We never understood where the merchants acquired it in the first place. Our driver would maneuver his vehicle down narrow streets and alleys littered with garbage and trash and then disappear into a nondescript doorway. He would soon return, followed by a little old man bent double under a tremendous sack of black wood. Unlike our U.S. charcoal, this stuff is composed of blackened fragments of wood carbonized to various degrees. It is often difficult to ignite, but once glowing, it produces a hot ember. Charcoal is used primarily in small amounts in water pipes in the smoking of tobacco, and it is expensive. We bought such large quantities that we had to go to a different merchant each day.

Since the earliest Egyptian breads were made from barley, which over time was gradually displaced by emmer, we needed some barley flour to try in various combinations with emmer. So we went to the seed souk. The aroma of every seed grown in the Middle East emanated from overflowing woven baskets that lined the street for blocks. We did find barley and then had to negotiate grinding it into flour. The scene could have come right out of the Middle Ages. The final step of separating the flour from the coarser particles was done by hand with a fine mesh tied over an oval hoop. We were intrigued by two goats that wandered back and forth during the milling process, stepping through and around the chaff as it piled up on the floor.

I had in mind something like Crisco to use for greasing the bread molds. I have no doubt that we could have found Crisco in Cairo, but trying to communicate that word to our driver didn't seem worth the effort. By various pantomimes we did get an idea across, which led us to a strange shop that had great piles of water buffalo fat. I bought lots of it. After similar adventures in finding white flour and sugar, we had acquired everything we needed.

In the meantime my Giza culture was growing by leaps and bounds. I had packed our baking supplies in Styrofoam containers, which I converted to proofing boxes. The hotel cleaning staff must have thought something very strange was going on in that room. Proofing boxes glowed from several spots, and every spare nook had a pail of culture bubbling away.

Finally, we could contain ourselves no longer. The bread molds weren't quite ready, but I had purchased four identical clay pots, far smaller than the bread molds, for the first attempts. I had also found one fairly large conical pot that closely resembled half of a bread mold. All were fired clay and didn't seem too porous, but I was concerned about the bread sticking, so I greased them heavily with the water buffalo fat, which seemed to disappear almost as fast as I applied it.

The bakery was finished, and we decided to christen it with our first experiment. We prepared enough dough, using the white flour culture, to fill two of the small pots and the larger conical one. The dough rose beautifully in the two small pots. It also rose in the larger one, but because of the increased volume it took longer. We let the dough rise to the top, used the two empty pots for lids on the smaller pots, leaving the larger uncovered, and heaped glowing charcoal around them. Half an hour went by with watchful waiting. Finally, a little smoke appeared to be coming from within the pots so I scraped the charcoal back a bit. More smoke. I moved the charcoal back some more and the smoke increased. All of a sudden the entire pot next to me burst into flames. The buffalo fat had seeped completely through the pot wall and ignited. The second pot followed the first, and for a few moments it looked like a misfired Fourth of July display. I finally managed to throw sand on the burning pots and eventually contained the dual blaze. Wearing heavy gloves, I grabbed the pots and moved them to the shelf formed by the low bakery wall. Then, with real trepidation, I pried off the lids. To our amazement things didn't look too bad. "Oven spring" had carried both loaves to the tops of the lids, and they were a pleasant brown. But the bottoms were cremated and had to be virtually cut loose. The contents of the larger pot, at first glance, looked like bread, but turned out to be doughy inside. We thought it was because the larger loaf hadn't had sufficient time to bake. As it turned out, we were wrong.

The team insisted on a taste test, so we cut our first "ancient" Egyptian bread from the small pots. It wasn't bad. It was distinctly sour, to be sure, because of the long incubation period of our culture caused by the various delays, but entirely edible and obviously bread. The dough had leavened exceptionally well—so well, in fact, that it misled us for a time. Perhaps the archaeologists were right and the dough would rise in the bread molds, filling both parts. Maybe the Egyptians did cut those loaves in half.

On that same day the bread molds were delivered and we were ready for another trial run. We started early the next morning, since we planned to fill a dozen molds. It was not a good day. The charcoal was reluctant to ignite, and the mass dough production took longer than anticipated. Fortunately, it again leavened in just under two hours, with the dough nearly to the top of the bottom sections of the molds. I carefully seated each dough-filled mold securely in a conical depression. Then I selected a top that fit (not all of them did). The last step was applying the charcoal. You can be sure I didn't put it quite as close as I had previously. Then I realized that when I placed the molds in their depressions, I hadn't put any charcoal under them. It seemed too late to reset the molds, so I decided to leave them as they were and see what would happen. What happened wasn't good. After about 90 minutes, I took off the lids, let the bread cool, and removed the loaves—well, part of the loaves. The tips that had been slightly underground were still unbaked dough, and that stayed in the molds.

Finally, the day of the photo shoot arrived. After the failures and successes of the experiments, I thought I knew how to do it. Our driver met us at 6:00 A.M. and by 7:00 we were at the bakery site. We used an emmer culture with various combinations of emmer and barley flour, and included a white flour culture with Kamut as a control of sorts. By 1:00 P.M. the molds were filled with dough and positioned on the bakery wall in a flat-bottomed holder and the dough was rising. Ken Garrett insisted that the sun needed to be low in the sky to produce the right lighting. So we timed the bread to be done at around 5:00 P.M.

At 2:00 P.M. the team gathered to offer their moral and physical support. I put them to work on a task that I hoped would change the theory of how Egyptians baked leavened bread. On the previous day Chris Sloan had spent hours developing a method for stacking the tops of the bread molds so they could be heated. I had been thinking about those tomb drawings that showed Egyptians stacking molds over heat in one scene and baking bread in another, and I had a theory I wanted to test. So the team stacked the empty molds over the searing heat of the charcoal. By 3:00 all of the doughs had risen as much as they were ever going to. We positioned the molds in their spots in the bakery floor, with a thin layer of glowing charcoal underneath, and placed a hot top from the stacked molds over each bottom. Next came the glowing charcoal at a safe distance around the molds. Positioned among the molds were two essential controls. One was a completely empty mold with a tiny hole in the heated top to permit us to monitor the temperature with the thermocouple. The other was a bottom mold filled with dough but lacking a top, which we hoped would help us understand the role of the tops. We banked a significant amount of charcoal against the bakery wall to reflect heat back against the molds.

The thermocouple gave us an early clue that we were doing something right. The temperature in the empty mold rose gradually to between 325° and 350°, perfect for bread, and stayed there. At the first sign of smoke coming from the molds, I scraped the charcoal farther away. By 4:30 the sun was going down and Garrett's shadows were appearing. It was show time! I pulled on my gloves and wrestled an emmer mold from the bed of smoking charcoal. Off came the lid, revealing a baked loaf of nicely browned emmer bread filling the bottom. I ran a slender knife blade around the inside of the mold, picked it up and with a quick shake evicted a gorgeous conical loaf showing only an occasional spot of early darkening from a little too much heat. It was just like the first leavened bread. The onlookers cheered. In quick succession the molds disgorged thirteen loaves of various combinations of flours. With the exception of the loaf made entirely from barley, all of the loaves were leavened to the top of the bottom part of the molds. All of the breads were proclaimed entirely edible by an enthusiastic audience, and the demonstration a complete success.

After all the breads had been removed and admired, there was still one bread mold in the bed of charcoal—the control without a top. I pushed the thermocouple probe deep into the loaf, and when it came out, soft bits of unbaked dough clung to it. The demonstration was complete: the top turned the mold into a sort of oven. Without this heated top, the bread did not bake.

CHAPTER 2

THE BIRTH AND LIFE OF SOURDOUGH

IT TOOK UNCOUNTED CENTURIES for wheat and other grains used for flour to evolve. Jarmo, in the uplands of Iraq, is one of the oldest archaeological excavations in the Middle East, dated to about 8000 B.C. Here archaeologists have identified carbonized kernels and clay imprints of plants that resemble wild and domesticated wheats. Historians believe that similar grains were established in Egypt by at least the same time, and perhaps as early as 10000 to 15000 B.C. Rye existed in the Middle East as an unwanted weed and eventually spread across the Mediterranean to the Baltic countries, where it dominates bread making to this day. These wild grasses took millennia to progress to grain-producing plants, and it was centuries before humans learned to cultivate and use them for food.

These grains were probably first consumed as porridge. Eventually, porridge evolved into a flat cake of baked cereal—baked perhaps on a hot rock in the fire. But how did these flat, hard cakes rise for the first time and become bread? An unbaked flat cake, perhaps forgotten on a warm summer evening, would be a perfect medium for contamination by an errant wild yeast. Imagine how many times that accident occurred before someone saw it and then baked it! It must have taken a thousand years, a thousand accidents, and finally a thousand experiments to produce a recognizable loaf of bread.

The Discovery of Yeast

In 1676 a Dutch lens grinder, Anton Van Leeuwenhoek, first observed and described microscopic life, and in 1680 he produced the first sketches of yeast in beer. But nothing more happened for the next 150 years. Yeast for bread was obtained from beer foam. This yeast was the first alternative to wild sourdough. Then came Louis Pasteur in 1857, with his proof that fermentation is caused by yeast. A comprehensive system of yeast classification, which we still use, was published in 1896.

With Pasteur's discovery, a whole new field of yeast technology and cereal chemistry sprang into life. Microbiologists learned how to isolate single yeast cells and to select pure cultures. They selectively bred the wild strains to develop yeasts that leavened faster, were more tolerant to temperature changes, and were easier to produce commercially. From these they mass-produced cakes of pressed yeast and packages of active dried yeast that contained billions of cells that were all exactly alike. These purified strains are now carefully guarded to prevent contamination by wild types. Cereal chemists learned to control the texture and appearance of bread by bleaching and blending different types of flour and found a host of chemical additives to improve the consistency of dough, change its flavor, increase the shelf life of the finished loaf, and improve its nutritional value. Agronomists selected and bred wheats that resist disease, produce bigger yields per acre, contain more protein, and so on. These advances all contributed to the industrial production of bread, with massive machines producing thousands of loaves per day. Now a handful of very large bakeries produce more than three-fourths of all bread sold in the United States. These same "advances" have also led to the flavor of modern bread being described as napkinlike.

Yeasts are microfungi, and are much larger than most bacteria. There are more than 350 different species, with countless additional strains and varieties. In the hundred or so years since Louis Pasteur discovered that yeast fermentation produces carbon dioxide, which leavens dough, yeasts have been studied by every conceivable technology and harnessed to perform hundreds of different tasks, from cleaning up oil slicks to producing antibiotics. Many are artificially produced for very specific functions, including commercially made bread.

It is important to understand the basic differences between the wild yeasts of sourdough and the commercial (baker's) yeast used in most other breads. Perhaps first is the fact that sourdough yeasts grow best in a slightly acid dough, while baker's yeast does better in a neutral or slightly alkaline one. Baker's yeast is represented by a single species, *Saccharomyces cerevisae*, while sourdoughs are usually leavened by multiple species in the same dough, none of which are baker's yeast. This mixture of yeast types contributes to the distinctive sourdough texture. Baker's yeast is a highly uniform product that produces an equally uniform texture in bread dough. The wild yeasts in sourdough are anything but uniform, and they vary from country to country. But the most impressive difference between the two types of yeast is that a single package of instant dried yeast produces just one batch of bread. The same amount of a wild sourdough culture produces loaf after loaf for many lifetimes of many bakers.

In 1 gram of commercial yeast there are 20 to 24 billion individual yeast cells; in a package of dry yeast there are 130 billion. By comparison, a cup of sourdough culture as it comes from the refrigerator contains far fewer yeast cells. The addition of baker's yeast to a sourdough culture poses the very real danger that the enormous number of commercial yeast cells may overwhelm the wild yeast and destroy the culture. In addition, you risk the introduction of a bacteriophage, or virus, to which the commercial cells are immune but that may kill the wild yeast. And if you leaven your dough with baker's yeast, the texture characteristic of sourdough will disappear. This book emphasizes repeatedly that you should never use baker's yeast either in your sourdough culture or in the recipe of your sourdough bread. *The secret of sourdough success lies in the art of stimulating that wild culture into a burst of reproductive activity to equal the numbers found in commercial yeast just before you use it in baking.* The steps of preparing the culture and performing the first proof, described at the beginning of Chapter 4, do just that!

The Role of Lactobacilli

Bakers of every sort welcomed the introduction of commercial yeast in the 1800s. It greatly simplified the baking process, and it made the process much faster. But something happened to the sourdough flavor. It disappeared!

In due time researchers identified the problem. They found that sourdough bread is the product of not one microorganism, but two. The wild yeast make it rise, and bacterial helpers produce the flavor. These beneficial bacteria are primarily lactobacilli, so named because they produce lactic acid, which contributes to the sour flavor. And they don't do it very fast. Experience has shown that the lactobacilli require approximately 12 hours to fully develop the authentic taste of sourdough. Extremely fast commercial yeasts, particularly active dry yeast, have shortened the rising process to 2 hours or less, hardly giving the lactobacilli a chance to get started.

Lactobacilli produce the flavor of sourdough breads by fermentation. That simple statement is the primary reason that sourdoughs are completely different from, and better than, most commercially produced breads. Fermentation is the process by which a variety of bacterial organisms act on food products to produce different flavors, textures, and aromas. Fermentation of milk produces butter and a host of cheeses, as well as yogurt, cottage cheese, sour cream, and buttermilk. Many types of sausage involve the fermentation of various meats. Fermentation is essential to produce many familiar vegetable foods, including pickles, sauerkraut, olives, and a host of dishes common in Europe and the Middle East. But few of us are aware that fermentation is essential to the flavor of sourdoughs. Without sufficient time for that process to occur, the flavor will be lost.

Lactobacilli that produce the famous taste of San Francisco sourdough have been studied by researchers in California. Additional studies have been reported on sourdoughs from Italy, the Middle East, India, and Germany. Unlike most bacteria, they thrive in the acid environment of sourdough and produce a variety of mild organic acids, alcohols, and countless additional compounds that are vital to the sourdough flavor. One researcher has listed no fewer than fifty-five separate compounds in fermented bread doughs, many of them, of course, present only in trace amounts. These fermentation products, particularly the organic acids, play an additional important role in preventing spoilage. As a result, sourdough breads have a much longer shelf life than that of most commercial bread. It is these microorganisms that make a Yukon bread taste different from a San Francisco bread, which is different from an Egyptian bread and, most certainly, different from any bread made with commercial yeast.

Research into Wild Sourdough Cultures

The research reported on bacteria that ferment bread is minuscule compared to the work on milk, meat, and vegetable fermentations. Although much of the research on other foods is not directly related to sourdoughs, many analogies are valuable in understanding the action of bacteria in bread doughs. Research on milk fermentation has identified a group of factors that inhibit the growth of starter bacteria in the production of cheese and yogurt. These inhibitors include antibiotics in the milk of cows treated to prevent udder infections. Sanitizers used in cleaning milking machines also sometimes find their way into milk. This is an important reason never to add anything to your sourdough culture except flour and water. Further, if you experience inconsistent results with recipes requiring milk, inhibitors of this type may be playing a role.

Scientists researching San Francisco sourdough observed that many bakeries in the area were using sourdough colonized by identical strains of yeast and lactobacilli. The widespread occurrence of these organisms was not because the bakeries shared their sourdoughs with one another, but because these organisms are dominant throughout the San Francisco area. This led scientists to name this strain of bacteria *Lactobacillus sanfrancisco*. The yeasts also have a common characteristic: they are unable to utilize maltose, one of the carbohydrates found in flour. This assumes special significance, since the lactobacilli require the maltose that the yeast doesn't use. There is also some evidence that the bacteria produce an antibiotic that protects the culture from contamination by harmful bacteria. In other words, the two organisms are mutually dependent; they have developed an extremely stable symbiotic relationship that has protected them for generations.

Sourdough research in Germany has also revealed the presence of different lactobacilli. It appears that sourdough cultures are colonized by the specific types of yeast and lactobacilli found where the cultures originate; this helps explain why breads from different areas often have such distinctive characteristics.

While directing the pathology department of a hospital laboratory in Saudi Arabia, I studied the microbiology of sourdough cultures my wife and I had collected during our travels. Each contained a dominant yeast accompanied by strains of lactobacilli. The yeast in each of the cultures revealed different physical characteristics under the microscope. I isolated both yeasts and bacteria in pure cultures, then recombined them to test the combination without interfering organisms. Detailed studies demonstrated that each culture represented a different yeast-lactobacillus combination. Each culture contained different combinations of wild yeast and two to four different bacterial strains. Our studies moved from the hospital laboratory to home kitchens, where thirty of our friends and associates tested the baking and taste characteristics. They helped to confirm that, indeed, each culture, whether it was from Bahrain or Saudi Arabia or San Francisco, produced remarkably different bread. Could one of them be the same combination that puzzled an Egyptian baker ten thousand years ago? We felt, at times, very close to that ancient Egyptian who first saw sourdough bubble.

CHAPTER 3

THE INGREDIENTS OF SOURDOUGH BREAD

FEW WOULD ARGUE THAT A GOOD, consistent culture (also known as a starter) is the single most essential ingredient for sourdough success. Wild cultures are mixtures of several strains of wild yeast and lactobacilli. Some leaven rapidly, some quite slowly. Some are very mild, others very sour. Some have a subtle flavor independent of the degree of sourness.

It is entirely feasible to capture your own culture simply by exposing a mixture of flour (I recommend starting with white flour and then transferring the culture to whichever flour is desired) and water to the air. Combine 2 cups of good-quality bread flour with 1¹/₂ cups of warm water in a 2-quart plastic, glass, or stainless steel bowl. Stir the mixture with sufficient vigor to beat in additional air. Expose the bowl and its contents to the air, preferably outside, although it can be done inside as well. Do not cover the bowl with plastic or anything that will exclude the organisms you are attempting to collect. If insects or other critters are a potential problem, cover the bowl with a fine-mesh screen or cheesecloth. Stir the mixture vigorously at least twice every 24 hours. In 2 or 3 days bubbles should appear on the surface as the first indication that you have been successful. Feed the culture an additional cup of flour and sufficient water to maintain the consistency, and stir it briskly again. You may need to repeat this additional feeding at 12-hour intervals for several successive days.

When you capture a yeast that is active enough to be useful, it will form a layer of foam 1 to 2 inches deep. If it doesn't attain this level of activity in 4 to 5 days, you should probably abandon the attempt and repeat the process in a different location. There are no guarantees, and you may encounter problems with contamination by undesirable organisms, particularly in areas with air pollution.

These organisms usually produce a bad odor or flavor, but are harmless. Once you have a good, bubbly culture, transfer it to one or more glass jars and refrigerate it. It is now ready for use. Don't freeze it.

The foam on top of a culture is evidence of wild yeast activity for leavening but is not indicative of the growth of lactobacilli needed for sourness and flavor. A multitude of methods have been suggested to ensure this bacterial component, most of them worthless. In the 1970s *Sunset* magazine recommended yogurt as a source of the lactobacilli that flavor yogurt. This method is not without hazard. The yogurt bacteria have been selected for their ability to metabolize the proteins of milk, not the starches of grain, so a stable, synergistic culture will not develop. Also, for good results, it is necessary to add milk as a nutrient. Milk occasionally contains antibiotics used to treat udder disease in cows or trace amounts of disinfectants used to sterilize milking equipment. Either may destroy the organisms of a sourdough culture. Other methods include using grapes or apples or potato water. All of these may result in lactobacilli, but they are no better than organisms collected from the air. The lactobacilli that grow in the simple mixture of flour and water are those that are capable of utilizing the starches present in flour and are more likely to form a symbiosis with the wild yeast, which will result in a culture with long-term stability.

There are several sources of wild sourdough cultures with demonstrated stability. The King Arthur Flour in Norwich, Vermont, supplies a moist culture, which they call a "classic New England" culture. My company, Sourdoughs International, in Idaho, offers a choice of ten cultures collected from around the world (see Chapter 7 for more information). These cultures are dried at low temperatures to preserve the viability of the organisms. Both moist and dried cultures must be activated by adding flour and water before use, as described on page 35. Activation may require 3 to 5 days. Once activated, all cultures should be refrigerated, not frozen. They are then ready for use after feeding and a short period of warming.

Flour

WHEAT BREAD FLOUR

Plant geneticists have produced a large number of wheat varieties designed for highly specific conditions and purposes, including soil type, growing temperatures, average rainfall, protein content, disease resistance, harvesting characteristics, yields per acre, and even adaptability to automated bread machines. These varieties fall into four major categories: hard and soft winter wheat and hard and soft spring wheat. Hard wheat has a "strong" gluten, which is required to trap the leavening gases and to form and maintain the shape of the bread loaf. Soft wheat has a "weak" gluten and is used to make various pastries, crackers, and similar products.

Spring wheat is planted in the spring and harvested in late summer. It is grown primarily in Montana, the Dakotas, Minnesota, and Canada, since the winters are often too cold in these areas for the wheat to survive if planted in the fall. It is known throughout the world as Manitoba or dark northern spring wheat and is considered to be the hardest wheat produced. Winter wheat is planted in the fall, lies dormant over the winter, and is harvested in early summer.

An additional variable is the method of milling, which is the grinding and sifting process that produces flour from grain kernels. During milling, the components of the kernel are separated, depending on the type of flour being produced. The largest portion of a wheat kernel is the endosperm, which contains about 75 percent of the kernel's protein and is the source of white flour. Bran is the outer coating of the kernel and is included in whole-wheat flour. The embryo or sprouting section of the seed is the germ. It contains fats and oils and is usually separated from flours, since it becomes rancid during storage.

In ancient times milling was done between two heavy stones, which not only removed the kernel's husk but ground the remaining portions so finely that they could not be separated. Some modern milling techniques still use special millstones, but the degree of fineness can now be regulated, and the kernel components can be separated. Some believe, however, that stone grinding of flour is done primarily for its image and promotional value. These flours are highly touted to the home baker, but the choice is largely one of personal preference. High-speed steel roller milling remains the most common method. The type of wheat is far more important to the sourdough baker than the milling process.

White flour is available in two major categories. Bleached flours are treated with chlorine compounds or other bleaching agents to whiten the flour and may also be treated with a number of chemical additives to improve baking characteristics. Unbleached flours generally have no chemical additives. Both are usually enriched, however, with iron and several of the B vitamins.

Hard spring wheats produce high-protein unbleached flours with strong gluten that need no additives to improve their performance. Lower-quality flours often require treatment with oxidizing agents to strengthen their gluten. They may be blended with several other flour types, and may even include barley. All-purpose flours are in this group.

Unfortunately, labels on flour rarely list the types of wheat. There is seldom a clue as to whether the wheat is hard or soft, winter or spring. In fact, most flours are a mixture of these types, but the proportions and types remain a mystery, or perhaps a secret. These blends and mixtures are ostensibly made to improve baking performance. It would appear they also are used to upgrade and utilize lesser types of flour. Grinding your own wheat is one way—perhaps the only way—to guarantee the type and quality of your flour and may offer a source of satisfaction as well.

The sourdough baker needs flour with a high protein content and strong gluten—a hard spring wheat is ideal. Old cookbooks advised buying such flour near where the wheat was produced to assure flour of a specific quality. That is hardly practical today. Wheat is shipped all over the world and is traded from country to country. The urban dweller is clearly at the mercy of the local supermarket. In the final analysis, one must depend on reliable brand names and experiment with various types of flour.

Avoid self-rising or instant flours, which may contain dried yeast or chemical leaveners or both. In general, 1 cup of self-rising flour contains 1½ teaspoons of leavening agent and ½ teaspoon of salt.

Whole wheat flours contain most of the components of the wheat kernel and are more nutritious than white flours. However, enrichment standards established by the FDA in the early 1940s for white flours have narrowed the nutritional differences between the two flour types. Whole wheat generally contains part or all of the wheat germ and will become rancid unless stored in the refrigerator or freezer. Most whole wheat flour is milled from selected hard spring wheat, so it is an excellent product for the sourdough baker. It is available in a variety of grinds, from very fine to very coarse. Cracked wheat is cut rather than ground and is used in bread recipes for special texture and flavor. Flaked and rolled wheats are also available.

KAMUT FLOUR

Kamut has an intriguing history that is shrouded in controversy. Some fifty years ago a serviceman stationed in Portugal was given a few grains of wheat said to be from King Tut's tomb. This "King Tut's grain" found its way to the Quinn

Egyptian bakers depicted
at work in 2575 B.C.

Egyptian bakers
making pita breads in
a primitive clay oven
in 1984 A.D.

Preheating the "ovens."

The author and Mark Lehner reproducing humankind's first leavened bread.

The finished product. Great flavor and nice crumb.

ranch in Montana, where it was planted and produced organically for a number of years. In the 1980s Bob Quinn studied the grain, classified it as *Triticum polonicum*, and gave it the trade name Kamut, an Egyptian word for wheat. Quinn believes it is unlikely that the grain could have survived in King Tut's tomb to germinate, but he says it may represent an isolated strain of ancient wheat perhaps still grown in small cultivars in Egypt. The grain is closely related to emmer, the great-grandfather of modern wheats, but unlike emmer, Kamut threshes free of its hull, making it a so-called naked wheat, like all modern wheats. Quinn continues to produce the grain organically on his Montana ranch but now markets it primarily through Arrowhead Mills in Texas and other outlets. It is widely available in nutrition and health food stores. It imparts a distinctive nutty flavor to sourdough bread.

SPELT FLOUR

Spelt may be even more ancient than Kamut and is said by some to have originated more than nine thousand years ago. It has been popular in Europe for thousands of years and is currently common in European food stores.

Like emmer, spelt has a tough husk that is difficult to remove, requiring special dehusking equipment. It was introduced to this country by Amish farmers in Ohio, who fed it primarily to livestock. In the 1980s Wilhelm Kosnopfl, then president of Purity Foods, financed a spelt research program at Ohio University and subsequently developed a facility at Okemos, Michigan, to provide spelt products to health food stores. In a conversation with Willy Kosnopfl early in 1996, he commented, "In Europe, spelt is used almost exclusively with sourdoughs." We both speculated that there may be something intrinsic about sourdough fermentation that makes it particularly well adapted to spelt flours.

The original marketing of spelt was a bit flamboyant, describing it as a nonwheat grain and therefore ideal for gluten-sensitive individuals. Most agronomists would disagree and consider spelt to be a distinct species of wheat. There is little general agreement on its allergenic properties.

Spelt is, however, a remarkable grain that produces terrific sourdough breads. The flour produces a soft, satiny dough with minimal kneading. Studies by a number of researchers seem to indicate that spelt gluten degrades rapidly during mixing, suggesting that mixing times should be limited for best results. Kneading does not appear to be affected, however, according to Don Stinchcomb, the current president of Purity Foods.

Most of my test baking is done with sourdough cultures grown in a mixture of white bread flour and water. For testing spelt flours, however, I transferred a Russian culture to a mixture of spelt and water so I could evaluate doughs made entirely of spelt. The results were impressive. The culture itself had an entirely different texture than that of a bread flour culture, almost like thick whipped cream. I baked recipes using 100 percent white spelt flour and mixtures of up to 68 percent whole spelt flour. The loaves uniformly leavened as well as doughs made with the same recipe using 100 percent white bread flour. I compared kneading for 5 minutes and 10 minutes and could detect no difference.

The product I evaluated is called Vita-Spelt and is produced by Purity Foods. It is advertised as organic, unenriched, unbleached, and unbromated, which in this era is pretty impressive. The breads I sampled were exquisite sourdoughs, and I have included several recipes for spelt breads in the next chapter.

If you want to make sourdough bread with 100 percent spelt, you should transfer your culture from a bread flour base to a spelt flour base. This is quite easy to do. If you are activating a dried culture, simply substitute white spelt flour for white bread flour. If you have an activated bread flour culture, put 1/4 cup into a quart Mason jar, add 1 cup of warm water, stir vigorously and add a cup of white spelt flour. Stir briefly and proof at 85° for approximately 12 hours. Then take 1/4 cup of this culture and repeat the process. After three or four repetitions you will have diluted the bread flour to an insignificant level.

Durum Flour

Discoveries are often made unexpectedly in strange places under peculiar circumstances. That is how I "discovered" durum. We all know, for example, that the best bread wheats are hard spring wheats with high protein, which means good gluten, right? Well, not necessarily. I found out differently when Pug, our great Brittany spaniel, got hurt. We named him Pug within hours after picking him out of a mass of puppies because, quite simply, he is pugnacious. Not mean, just very determined.

I had always thought durum was a wheat used almost exclusively to produce pastas. Since noodles are soft, I assumed that durum was a soft wheat. I never heard of anyone using durum to bake bread.

My enlightenment on the subject of durum came during a hunting trip. Pug is a hunting breed—a pointer—and he had taken my wife and me to North Dakota to hunt pheasants. We were hunting in some very thick cover where it was difficult to see the dog, and he disappeared for about 15 minutes. When we saw him next, our hearts dropped. Even from a distance we knew something was very wrong by the way he was moving and dragging his head through the brush. As he came closer, we could see he was severely injured. His face, jaws, mouth, tongue, chest, and front legs were an absolute mass of deeply embedded porcupine quills. We soon determined that it would be virtually impossible for the two of us to restrain him sufficiently to remove even a fraction of the barbed spikes. We were a long way from any town or city and had no idea where to find the nearest veterinarian. We stopped at the first farm for information and met a true gentleman who from that point on has affected our lives greatly.

Arlen Gilbertson told us that the nearest vet was more than 75 miles away. He also said that he and his son, with our help, could do the job if we had the stomach for it. We gratefully accepted the offer. By the time we finished, we knew quite a lot about each other. Arlen has spent all his life on the North Dakota farm started by his father. Together they have raised primarily durum for several decades.

In the months that followed, we stayed in touch and I learned a lot about durum from a man who knows a lot about it and is proud of the crop he grows. He would hold a grain between his fingers and point out that it was almost transparent. Then he'd tap it with a hammer to demonstrate its hardness. It is a spring wheat, and when he told me the protein content was between 14 and 17 percent, I began to get interested. I wondered why no one was making bread with it. Did that high protein mean high gluten? When I left for Idaho, I had a sack of Arlen's durum. When I got home I ground it into flour.

The first baking trials were disappointing. At a level of 25 percent durum, there was a definite reduction in leavening, but the flavor was exceptionally good. I couldn't understand why a hard wheat with a high percentage of protein wouldn't have good gluten. To my surprise, Arlen didn't know either, but he knew someone who could answer any question about durum. Following his advice, I contacted Dr. Elias Elias in the Department of Plant Sciences at North Dakota State University. Dr. Elias is an assistant professor and durum wheat breeder. He had lots of answers and information. He told me that all glutens are not alike. Durum wheats and their glutens have been selected to produce the qualities in pastas that have made North Dakota durums famous worldwide, but those glutens are not noted for their leavening qualities, as other wheat glutens are. Further, there is no direct relationship between gluten quality and percentage of protein. That is, a high level of protein is not always associated with good-quality gluten, and a low level of protein may have good gluten. Then he told me something that very few people seem to know about. For the last 20 years, plant breeders at North Dakota State University have been working to develop strains of durum with improved gluten (and other characteristics). Dr. Elias graciously sent me the description of four new durum varieties named Renville, Monroe, Vic, and Munich, the latter still in review in late 1995. All four have significantly improved gluten over former strains. He suggested that I contact Dr. LeRoy Spilde, director of Foundation Seedstocks at the university, and inquire if any samples of the new strains were available for test baking experiments. I did so, and within a week 10 pounds of Renville durum were delivered to my door. All this because a durum farmer took the time to help an injured Brittany. And you don't believe in serendipity?

I have conducted a number of tests with Renville, and you will be hearing more about this remarkable grain and its siblings for making bread of every kind. Its baking characteristics are nearly equal to the best bread flours, and in one way it is far superior: It has an extraordinary flavor. In my baking trials I used a standard recipe consisting only of flour, a sourdough culture, salt, and water to avoid introducing masking flavors. The results were so outstanding that I had difficulty protecting the Renville loaves long enough to take photographs.

When I told Dr. Elias of my results, he wasn't the least bit surprised. He told me that he had grown up in Syria, where most of their bread is made from durum; he said he knows how good it is. I had called him primarily to find out how the American consumer can get a good-quality durum for home bread baking, because I hadn't found any in Idaho. The answer wasn't good. If you're in North Dakota, stop at any farm or mill and you can usually buy durum grain at almost give-away prices. If you're not in North Dakota, ask your local supplier to locate a source. It may not be easy, but if enough of us start searching, it will soon be on the shelves. It's worth a lot of searching! If you can't find it anywhere, contact me and I'll find a source for you.

RYE FLOUR

Rye grain is grown mainly in the Dakotas, Minnesota, and Nebraska, in soils requiring hardy grain varieties. It is a winter grain, planted in the fall and harvested the following summer. Rye protein is not of the gluten-forming type, and breads made entirely with rye flour do not rise well. It is usually mixed with wheat flour to produce a lighter loaf with the rye flavor. Sourdough cultures originating in central Europe, where rye has been a dominant grain for centuries, may be better adapted to fermenting rye doughs. When rye is milled, two basic types of flour are produced: white and dark. White rye flour is made only from the endosperm. It is particularly recommended for mildly flavored Jewish and other light rye breads. It is generally mixed with 60 to 70 percent good-quality white flour. Dark rye is a more distinctive-flavored dark flour especially adapted for heavy, dark rye breads such as German, Swedish, and pumpernickel. It is usually mixed with about 80 percent high-protein white flour or whole wheat flour. Pumpernickel is a coarse, dark rye flour made by grinding the entire rye kernel. It is analogous to whole wheat and is milled in fine, medium, and coarse pumpernickel flours. Rye blends are also available that combine regular or dark rye with a good-quality high-protein white flour.

Wheat Gluten

Arrowhead Mills produces a product called Vital Gluten that is quite useful for increasing the leavening potential of gluten-deficient flours such as the rye varieties. Other mills sell a similar product simply labeled "gluten flour." Gluten is extracted from wheat flour through a water washing procedure, yielding a fine, white concentrated gluten. Arrowhead recommends 1½ teaspoons per cup for whole-grain breads. It is especially useful in bread machines if adequate leavening is a problem.

Water

One seldom has control over one's source of water. Fortunately, water quality rarely poses a problem. Medium-hard water is perhaps best. It is said that soft water results in sticky doughs that are difficult to handle. But we have even used distilled water on occasion and found it difficult to detect any difference in dough consistency. Extremely alkaline water, however, will inhibit wild yeast activity and result in poor leavening. Contrary to considerable printed advice, trace metals usually have no deleterious effect, nor do fluoride additives. High iron concentrations also are of no consequence. One potential problem is chlorine. We have never had a problem using chlorinated water, but others have reported that avoiding water with chlorine has solved problems with their sourdough baking.

Salt

Salt has a stabilizing effect on yeast fermentation and a toughening effect on gluten. It is, incidentally, a required dough constituent under FDA standards, although salt-free bread is permitted for individuals on low-sodium diets. Almost all recipes in this book specify 1 or 2 teaspoons of salt, but it is not an essential ingredient.

Milk

Most commercially baked white breads in the United States are made with some form of milk, usually nonfat dried milk. In fact, the baking industry is the largest single consumer of this product in the country. Dried buttermilk, dried whole milk, and several whey products are also used in commercial breads. The home baker has any number of types of dried and fresh milk available. The recipes in this book that call for milk all use 2 percent (low-fat) milk, but almost any milk or milk substitute is acceptable. Remember, milk may contain antibiotics and trace amounts of disinfectants used to sterilize milking equipment. These contaminants may kill the organisms in your sourdough culture. Do not use milk as a replacement for water in the culture.

Fats

Lard, butter, oils, and margarine can generally be used interchangeably. Vegetable oils are convenient to use, but many bakers believe butter gives a better loaf texture. Fats and oils increase loaf volume, prevent crust cracking, enhance keeping qualities, and improve slicing qualities (the crumb).

Sweeteners

When a recipe lists sugar, most bakers use white sugar. But many other sweeteners can be substituted, including corn syrups and honey. Sugar is a yeast nutrient, although its primary function in bread making is to influence flavor. Yeasts use the carbohydrates and starch in flour as their primary energy source, and too much sugar will actually inhibit, not stimulate, yeast fermentation.

Personalizing Breads

Today's baker has a delicious selection of specialty baking ingredients available from around the world. From gourmet shops and health food stores one can get exotic spices, unusual flours, foreign nuts and berries, seeds, cheeses, and flavorings that make bread variations almost endless.

One of the major advantages of doing your own baking is your ability to adjust the recipes to your own health standards. High-fiber grains such as oats may be added to many of the recipes. Steel cut oats, for example, produce a unique texture and distinctive flavor. To eliminate cholesterol, oil may be substituted for butter. You can also experiment with omitting eggs. Many people who once enjoyed baking bread have given it up because the temptation of hot bread was too hard on their diets. However, a slice of most home-baked sourdough breads contains no cholesterol and less than 150 calories. For a healthful, high-calorie, high-energy snack for kids, athletes, and backpackers, add nuts, seeds, raisins, dates, wheat germ, and anything else you want. The loaf will be heavy but durable.

 CHAPTER 4

PUTTING IT ALL TOGETHER

I T IS DIFFICULT TO BUY A LOAF of sourdough bread that isn't flavored with vinegar or a variety of chemicals to simulate the real thing. But we can bake it in our kitchen just as our ancestors did for thousands of years. With a sourdough culture, a recipe, flour, and water, the sourdough breads of history and the world are at our fingertips.

Using the Recipes

When I wrote the first edition of this book, I felt that the instructions for culture preparation and the first proof were so important that I repeated them at the beginning of each recipe. They are still crucial, but to eliminate repetition, I have described them at length here, and, for quick reference, at the beginning of the recipe section, and have omitted them from the recipes themselves. Culture preparation produces that one most essential ingredient: a fully activated culture. The first proof utilizes that culture for 12 hours of intense fermentation to transform several cups of flour into a mass of pure sourdough, the nucleus of everything you bake.

First, some quick words on terminology. Throughout this book you will see the term "proof." Many bread recipes in other cookbooks have a short proofing step merely to test the potency of commercial yeast. I use the term to refer to the process by which yeast ferments flour and water to produce dough and later to make the dough rise. Longer "proofs" will produce a different texture or flavor by allowing the yeast and bacteria more time for fermentation.

Many bakers and authors refer to their sourdough cultures as "starters," since a small amount of pure culture is always retained to start the next batch. I use the two terms interchangeably.

Many of the recipes specify warm water or milk. This means any temperature between 75° and 85°. Hotter water may endanger the yeast; colder water will slow the leavening process.

The amounts of flour and water listed in the various proofs and recipes are specified primarily as guidelines for the beginner. With experience, the baker judges these ingredients more by the consistency of the dough (with baking machines this is essential). If it is too dry or stiff, add more water. If too thin, add more flour. Perhaps the loaves will be a little larger or a little smaller, but the differences will be insignificant.

Activating Cultures

In Chapter 3, I described how to capture your own culture. If you follow this route, you can skip this step. If you have obtained a dried or moist culture, you must activate it before baking with it. The initial activation may require several days, as the organisms are dormant. This process may seem a little tedious, but once it is completed your culture will function forever. When activated, the culture may be used at once or refrigerated for later use. If refrigerated, it must be fed and warmed briefly before use, as described in the next step, culture preparation.

The initial activation of both dried and moist cultures is essentially the same, although moist cultures may activate somewhat faster than dried ones. Place the entire contents of one package in a container. We recommend a 1-quart wide-mouth canning jar (page 44). Add 1 cup white bread flour and ³/₄ cup of warm (75° to 85°) water, mix well, and proof in a warm place for 24 hours. Stir the culture vigorously several times during this period. Place the lid on the jar, but do not tighten it.

At the end of 24 hours, the culture will begin to show a few small bubbles The amount of time will depend on the culture. Feed the culture an additional cup of flour and sufficient water to maintain the consistency and repeat vigorous stirring to whip additional air into the mixture. Repeat this feeding and stirring process at approximately 12-hour intervals until the culture forms a 1- to 2-inch layer of foam on the surface, at which time it is ready to use or to refrigerate for later use.

Some cultures will fully activate in 24 to 48 hours, while others may require 3 to 5 days. When your jar is two-thirds full, pour half into another jar and feed both until activated. Keep the second jar as a backup in case some accident destroys one of them. Once activated, very fast cultures may reach their peak activity in 2 to 4 hours, exhaust the flour nutrients, and become semidormant almost as fast. If you do not look at the culture for 8 to 12 hours, you may miss this peak activity, and the culture may appear "flat," leading you to believe that activation has not occurred. Usually "tracks" of foam left on the inside of the jar by the rising and falling layer of bubbles will lead to the correct conclusion. A layer of clear brown fluid on the surface, called the "hooch," is normal and indicates that the culture is active. This fluid should be retained and stirred back into the culture.

If you have several dry cultures and do not plan to activate all of them right away, store them in your refrigerator, not your freezer.

Step 1: Culture Preparation

The single most important consideration for success in sourdough baking is to start with a fully activated culture. If you are beginning with a refrigerated culture, this step will reactivate the culture and get it ready for use. With an aggressive, active culture (the Russian culture available from Sourdoughs International [page 176], for example) that is used two or three times a week, this step can be omitted. With slower cultures or any culture not used at least every two weeks, culture preparation is an important first step each time you bake.

When sourdough cultures are refrigerated, the yeast cells go into a resting or lightly dormant stage. When the culture is warmed, the yeast begin to multiply if nutrients (flour) are provided. The time required for a culture to become fully active varies with the strain of yeast, how often it is used, and the temperature.

Remove the culture from the refrigerator and "feed" it 1 cup of flower and $^3/_4$ cup of warm (75° to 85°) water. I do this step right in the jar in which it was stored. Mix briefly. The mixture need not be lump-free as the yeast will digest any small lumps present. Warm the culture in a proofing box (page 40) or any warm area (85° to 90°). After 6 to 12 hours, the yeast cells will be actively multiplying. When you plan on baking, it is usually most convenient to do this step in the morning of the day before you actually bake. By evening, the fully active culture will be ready for the first proof, as evidenced by a layer of foamy bubbles. If you don't see that foam or "tracks" left by the rising and falling culture on the inside of the jar, it is wise to repeat the process and put off your baking until you are convinced that the culture is fully activated.

Step 2: The First Proof

With an activated culture you are ready to start the first proof, which will last about 12 hours. During this time the lactobacilli produce the unique sourdough flavor that can be obtained in no other way. At the same time the yeast continues to multiply, starts to produce the gases that will leaven the dough, and conditions the gluten to trap those gases. Many bakers refer to the dough at this stage as the "sponge."

Use a 4-quart mixing bowl, as the dough will at least double in volume. Place the culture in the bowl, and add 2 cups warm water; mix briefly. This will result in a more even dispersion of the culture as the flour is added. Then add 3 cups flour, a cup at a time, mixing briefly between cups. Again, the mixture need not be lump-free. Cover the bowl with a dry cloth or plastic wrap. Do not use a damp cloth, as the evaporation will cool the culture. Place in a proofing box or other warm location for approximately 12 hours. In general, a shorter fermentation will produce a milder flavor and a longer one a stronger or more sour flavor. Some fast cultures may use all the nutrients and become semidormant in this 12-hour time. See the section on Leavening Problems, page 39, to correct this problem. If the sponge retracts a bit, there may be some dried crust on the surface and on the sides of the bowl. Stir all of this into the dough before proceeding to the second proof.

Two things are essential. Before you remove some of the sponge to save as the culture for next time, don't add *anything* except flour and water. In particular, never add baker's yeast or milk. At the end of the first proof, return at least 1 cup of the culture, or whatever is left over from the recipe, to a clean culture container before starting the second proof. (If you feed this with a cup each of flour and water and leave it in a warm place for an hour before refrigerating, it will be easier to reactivate the next time.) These precautions will keep your wild culture free of contamination from the other ingredients of bread and will maintain a pure culture for future use.

If you want to get into some advanced baking techniques proposed by my friend Bob Linville, add to the sponge flavorful seeds (such as fennel or caraway) called for in the recipe you plan to make, to give their flavors longer to permeate the dough. *Be sure to save some culture for next time before adding these ingredients.*

Step 3: The Second Proof

Now you are ready to make the dough with the recipe you have chosen and form the loaves. However, if you are using a very fast culture, feed the dough 1 cup flour and ¾ cup water 2 hours before proceeding. See the section on Leavening Problems (page 39). Combine all of the liquids, including the oils or melted butter. Warm the mixture (to less than 85° to 90°), add salt and sugar (if specified by the recipe), and stir briefly until dissolved. The milk can be warmed in the microwave and the butter added and melted. Two minutes on defrost works well in most microwaves. Add this mixture to the culture from the first proof and mix well. This ensures a better distribution of these components throughout the dough. Then add the remaining dry ingredients, including spices, raisins, and special flours, and mix thoroughly. Finally, add the white flour, a cup at a time, until the mixture is too stiff to beat by hand. Turn the dough onto a floured surface and knead until smooth and satiny (see Kneading, page 41). Kneading completes the formation of gluten, which is essential to trap the gases formed by yeast during the leavening process. At this point many bakers let the dough proof for an additional 2 to 4 hours, punch it down, and let it rise another 30 minutes before forming the loaves. Many wild yeasts, however, will not be capable of producing sufficient gas to leaven the dough twice. Therefore, as soon as kneading is completed, form the loaves and allow them to rise.

Turn the dough onto a floured surface and form the loaves (see Forming Loaves, page 42). Place the loaves in nonstick loaf pans or on nonstick baking sheets (grease pans or sheets if not nonstick) and proof them for 2 to 3 hours. Cover them lightly with a dry cloth or plastic to prevent excessive drying. A tough, dry skin will inhibit rising. When they have doubled in bulk, or have risen an inch or two above the rim of the pans, they are ready for baking.

Step 4: Baking

Baking times and temperatures are specified in the recipes. Preheat the oven to the desired temperature before starting to bake. This makes the trapped gases expand rapidly and creates "oven spring" as the loaves suddenly increase in volume. Since oven thermostats are often inaccurate, it is advisable to check the temperature with an oven thermometer. At higher elevations it may be necessary to increase the temperature and time of baking. For example, at 7,500 feet increase the baking temperature by 25° and the time by 10 minutes. The best way to determine the time required for your oven is by inserting a digital thermometer into the center of the loaf when you remove it from the oven. The interior temperature should be 190°.

After taking the bread out of the oven, remove it from the pan and allow it to cool on a wire rack. If left in the pan, it will become moist and soggy. Most breads should not be sliced until 15 to 20 minutes after being taken from the oven, to achieve the best texture.

Helpful Hints

Don't get hung up on the mathematics. Sourdoughs by hand are much more tolerant than sourdoughs in machines. Sometimes you'll end up with an extra ½ cup of culture or perhaps flour. Don't hesitate to add it to the dough. It may make the loaves a little bigger, but they will taste just as good, maybe better. You will note that many of the recipes require 4 cups of culture. It is wise to save any additional culture that accumulates during the activation stage in a second jar to create a backup culture just in case you need more or make an irreversible error and bake everything.

Leavening Problems

It seems ironic, but our fastest culture, the Russian culture, creates most of the leavening problems. When fully activated, this culture reaches its peak leavening activity in less than 3 hours and then becomes semidormant almost as fast. If the first proof lasts 12 hours (which it must if the lactobacilli are to have sufficient time to produce the full sourdough flavor), the Russian yeast will have reached their peak, exhausted the nutrients in the flour, and assumed a resting stage. If you continue on to the second proof at this point, the dough will have a fine flavor, but it will not start to rise for another 3 hours, or until the culture again regains its peak activity. The solution is relatively simple: two or three hours before you make up the loaves, add a cup of flour to the dough, with sufficient water to maintain the consistency, and mix briefly. This will reactivate the wild yeast, and when the loaves are made, they will rise well and taste great.

Proofing Temperatures

Most recipes in this book call for a proofing temperature of 85°. To produce actively multiplying yeast cells, a temperature between 85° and 90° is highly desirable. Any warm area in this temperature range will suffice. However, if you place loaves or rolls near a warm stove, they will rise faster on the side nearest the heat and will be misshapen unless your rotate them occasionally. Many ovens set at "warm" are satisfactory, but be sure to check it with a thermometer. If the temperature is too high (above 100°), it will kill the culture; if it is too low (below 70°), many wild yeasts will not multiply.

Proofing Boxes

You can make a proofing box from an inexpensive Styrofoam ice chest to accurately regulate the temperature without having to heat an entire room. Obtain a chest large enough to fit upside down over your large mixing bowls (the lid is not used). Run a wire through the bottom of the ice chest, attach it to a porcelain light bulb socket, and screw this socket to the middle of the inside of the bottom of the chest. By experimenting, you can determine the correct bulb wattage to maintain a temperature of 85° when the chest is placed upside down over your mixing bowl filled with dough. A 15-watt bulb is usually satisfactory. If the temperature is too high, raise the chest an inch or less above the table. Use an accurate thermometer to determine the final temperature. Some innovative bakers use a dimmer switch on the electric cord to regulate the temperature exactly. A simple handle from a hardware store screwed to the outside of the bottom (now the top) of the box facilitates handling.

Kneading

More has probably been written about kneading than about any other aspect of bread making. A few caveats: it is difficult to do wrong, it is difficult to do too much, and it takes a little experience to become comfortable doing it and knowing when to quit. Most of us enjoy kneading. It's one of those mind-releasing exercises that contributes to the overall satisfaction of making bread. And it is certainly easier to work stiff dough with your hands than it is with a large spoon. Kneading should begin when the dough becomes too stiff to handle easily with a spoon and starts to fall away from the sides of the bowl. Turn it out onto a floured board. Every baking book says to knead on "a well-floured board." With sourdoughs, which sometimes are a little sticky, "well floured" means just that. I frequently use an entire cup to cover the bread board before turning the dough out of the bowl. This extra flour is very helpful as you gather the soft dough, form a loose ball, and start to knead. Work the dough back and forth with the ball and heel of your hand. Flatten the dough and fold the far edge over to fill in the depression, then push down on the doubled part. Between each push, rotate the dough about a quarter turn, so that it all gets an equal share of kneading. As you push back and forth, the dough will pick up flour from the board and your hands. As it becomes sticky, add more flour to the dough. If necessary, sprinkle more flour on the board. Continue until the dough no longer picks up flour from the board and begins to stiffen perceptibly. It will develop a satiny sheen and a smooth texture. If the dough is not stiff enough, it will droop and fall over the edge of the pan as it rises, and French loaves will spread sideways, producing a flat loaf instead of a plump one. If it is too stiff and dry, the loaves will split as they rise, allowing the leavening gases to escape prematurely. Can you knead too much? Probably not if you are doing it by hand.

You can overknead if you are using a power mixer, however. The dough will "slacken," and the resulting gluten will be of poor quality, letting a portion of the leavening gases escape. Power mixers and food processors vary markedly in their ability to handle sourdoughs, which are far more tenacious than bread doughs made with commercial yeast. Follow the instructions for your mixer carefully, but don't be surprised if sourdoughs overload your mixer. I have even experienced significant problems with good, heavy-duty equipment.

Forming Loaves

Like kneading, there are different ways to form dough into loaves, and most of them work. The objective is to produce a loaf that is round, oval, oblong, or some other shape with a skin that won't let the leavening gases escape as the loaf rises. To start, form the dough into a ball. This can be patted or pushed directly into the desired shape. I pat or roll the ball into a flat oval about 1 inch thick and then either fold it in half and pinch the two edges together or roll the dough up, pinching the seam together occasionally as the roll progresses.

You can cut a pattern in the loaf just before putting it in the oven. Using a razor blade that is sharp enough to cut through the unbaked crust without tearing, make cuts about ⅛ to ¼ inch deep. If you slash the loaf before it begins to rise, some of the gases will escape and the slashes will become quite wide as the loaf expands. However, there are no limits on artistic license.

In extremely dry areas, the skin that forms as the loaves rise may be so tough that it limits the desired expansion. You can increase the humidity by placing a glass of hot water in the proofing box and replacing it occasionally as it cools. It may also be desirable to place a pan of hot water in the oven during the first 10 minutes of baking to soften the crust and assist the oven spring as the gases expand from the heat.

Crust Texture

The texture of the crust can be modified by different treatments before and during baking. Brushing the loaves with cold water just before baking will produce a harder crust. French breads usually have a chewy crust, which is produced by placing a shallow pan of boiling water in the oven for the first 10 minutes to simulate a steam oven. I spray loaves and the oven with water, using a mister, several times at 5-minute intervals just as baking starts, and the crusts are really terrific! A softer crust will result if you brush the loaves with melted butter or oil before baking.

For a glossy, hard coating, mix 1 teaspoon cornstarch in ¹/₂ cup water. Heat the water to boiling, then cool and brush it onto the loaves just before baking. A glaze made from a well-beaten egg produces a golden brown crust. For a deep brown, try brushing the unbaked loaves with milk. Any of these glazes can be used just before baking and once or twice during baking, if desired. Crusts sometimes split as the loaves rise. This lets the gases escape and limits the desired expansion of the loaf. The cause is either too much flour, creating an overly dry dough, or, more commonly, poor bread flour with weak gluten.

Freezing and Thawing

Baked sourdough breads maintain their flavor, aroma, and freshness very well when frozen for several months. As soon as they are completely cooled, double-wrap the loaves in plastic and aluminum foil, and place them in the freezer. To thaw a frozen loaf, unwrap it and place it in an oven preheated to 350° for 15 minutes, or microwave on high for 4 minutes, rotating frequently.

Utensils

Some bakers advocate using wooden spoons to mix dough to avoid contamination with toxic trace metals. With modern utensils, this is unlikely to occur. Wooden spoons are pleasant to grip but are difficult to use for heavy mixing as they frequently snap at the handle. Large stainless mixing spoons are well suited to the job, but individual preference will dictate your choice.

In addition to the usual glass or ceramic mixing bowls, stainless steel or aluminum mixing bowls are acceptable. They do not contaminate sourdoughs during the mixing or proofing periods. Heavy-duty plastic bowls are also very satisfactory.

Loaf pans and baking sheets come in every size and shape. I use metal pans with a nonstick surface. They do not need to be greased before each use. If you use glass baking pans, reduce the oven temperature by 25°. The recipes in this book uniformly use 9 × 5 × 3-inch loaf pans when the recipe calls for 6 cups of flour in all. For smaller loaves using about 4 cups flour, use 8$\frac{1}{2}$ × 4 × 2$\frac{1}{2}$-inch pans. In the smaller pans, reduce baking time by 10 minutes.

Culture Containers

Long-term storage of a mildly acid culture in a metal container may cause leaching of toxic ions and adversely affect the culture. Any glass, ceramic, or plastic container is acceptable if it is big enough and has a loose-fitting but relatively secure lid. Wide-mouth quart canning jars are ideal because they are big enough to hold a bit more than 3 cups of culture, have a loose-fitting lid, and are relatively inexpensive. The lids should be replaced periodically if they become etched or if the rubber seals deteriorate. Don't tighten the lids of the containers, since the cultures can build up pressure, particularly if the temperature goes up, and fracture the jars.

Contrary to popular belief, sourdough containers should be cleaned regularly. After the culture preparation step, if you use all of the culture in the first proof, this is a good time to completely clean the container. After many weeks of storage in the refrigerator, containers build up a residue of dried culture and sometimes of mold.

Care and Feeding of a Heritage Sourdough

Your sourdough culture may be one, a hundred, or a thousand or more years old, and it cannot be easily destroyed except by too much heat. Always refrigerate a culture when it is not being used. If you don't, the organisms may completely utilize all of the available nutrients (flour) and perish from starvation. Do not freeze your cultures, as the wild yeast may not survive freezing and thawing.

Many home bakers use more than one sourdough culture and worry that one may contaminate and displace the organisms of the others. In general, I don't believe this is a significant problem. Stable cultures are characterized by organisms that have become dominant over extremely long periods of time with symbiotic relationships that are difficult to disrupt. In spite of this, however, you should use some precautions to prevent gross contamination. Do not bake with different cultures at the same time. Avoid contaminating the culture with commercial yeasts or chemical leaveners. The symbiosis between wild yeast and lactobacilli is very stable, but it can be destroyed by man-made yeast mutants or chemicals. Don't risk it by adding them to your culture. Ironically, commercial bakers have just the opposite concern: they take extreme measures to prevent the contamination of their cultures with wild yeast. Do not mix scraps or leftovers from bread dough into your culture. The effect of salt, sugar, spices, and other ingredients on wild yeast is unpredictable and therefore undesirable.

When a culture is placed in the refrigerator, the yeast become dormant. After extended refrigeration, some of the yeast cells will be damaged and die. It is desirable to have a high concentration of active yeast at the start of cooling to produce a maximum number of cells that will regenerate the culture when it is warmed. At the end of the first proof, feed the culture with 1 cup flour and ³/₄ cup of water and then proof it for 1 hour at 85° before returning it to the refrigerator. The consistency of the culture should be similar to thick pancake batter. If it becomes thicker, add a little water. If it is too thin, add flour.

In spite of all care, the culture is contaminated every time it is used, by the flour that is added. Regardless of how flour is manufactured, it contains some natural bacteria and molds. When the culture is dormant, under refrigeration, these organisms may overcome the protection that the yeast and lactobacilli produce for each other and form mold on the surface. If this occurs, simply remove most of the offending material, transfer the culture to a clean container, add flour and water, and warm to 85°. In 6 to 24 hours the culture will reestablish its symbiosis and the contamination will be gone. On rare occasions it may be necessary to repeat the process two or three times until the original culture takes over. It is normal for a brownish liquid, the "hooch," to form on top of the culture. This is a mixture of organic alcohols formed during fermentation and has no adverse effect. Just mix it into the culture before using.

After long periods of refrigeration, the number of viable yeast cells may be very small. Add flour and water and proof for 24 hours. Then pour off half the mixture, discard it, and again add flour and water. Repeating this process several times will also dilute the metabolic products that have accumulated over a long period of time (even at low temperatures) and that may be inhibitory to the culture. Old-timers called this "sweetening the pot." Similarly, after extended periods of very frequent use, a culture can become overly acidic and inhibited. Sweetening the pot will restore the balance and be very therapeutic. I am frequently asked how often a culture must be fed to maintain its viability. Is it necessary to have a baby-sitter feed it when you take a month of vacation? Stable cultures should survive easily for at least six months without feeding if refrigerated.

CHAPTER 5

RECIPES

ALL OF THE WORLD SOURDOUGH CULTURES described in Chapter 7 and available from Sourdoughs International, when used with these recipes, produce unique breads with distinctive flavors and textures. Some leaven much faster than others. The Russian culture and the Egyptian culture from the Red Sea leaven very rapidly and are quite mild. The San Francisco, Yukon, French, and Giza cultures leaven at moderate rates and are moderately sour. The cultures from Bahrain and Austria leaven somewhat more slowly and are more sour. The Saudi and Finnish cultures have the most distinctive flavors. You can vary the flavor and sourness of all the cultures by decreasing or increasing the length of the first proof.

As sourdough bakers we are most concerned with sourness and leavening. Lactobacilli in the culture produce the sour taste, which can be increased by prolonging the first proof. The wild yeast regulate the texture and leavening; the key here is to have the yeast at its peak of activity when starting the second proof. Essential for both yeast and the lactobacilli is a sufficiently warm temperature and an adequate supply of flour nutrients.

Culture preparation and the first proof are a part of every recipe. To reduce repetition, I have given brief instructions for each of these steps here and omitted them from the recipes. (A longer description of the process is given on pages 36–38.)

Culture Preparation

1. Remove the culture from the refrigerator. Add 1 cup white bread flour and $^3/_4$ cup warm water to the culture jar and mix briefly. It need not be lump-free.

2. Proof at 85° for 3 to 8 hours (this will vary, depending on culture) until the culture is actively fermenting, as shown by bubbles on the surface.

First Proof

1. Mix 2 cups of the active culture with 3 cups flour and 2 cups warm water in a 4-quart mixing bowl. It need not be lump-free.

2. Proof for about 12 hours.

Second Proof and Baking

1. Measure out the amount of culture called for in the recipe, and place it in a large mixing bowl. Return the remaining culture to a clean culture container and refrigerate.

For the second proof and baking, follow the directions given with each recipe.

World Bread

Makes 2 loaves

This recipe provides an introduction to wild sourdoughs for novice and experienced baker alike. Once you have mastered it, you will be ready to experiment with any recipe that follows. World Bread will convince you and any other skeptics that all sourdough cultures are not the same. It is a basic recipe used throughout the world. The culture you choose will give the bread its flavor and texture. If you are interested in using the recipe to compare different cultures, try to eliminate all other variables. Be sure the proofing times are identical. Then set up a taste panel of your friends and neighbors as judges. Code the loaves so the tasters are not influenced by the source or name of the culture.

4 cups culture from the first proof (page 37)
2 tablespoons butter
1 cup milk
2 teaspoons salt
2 tablespoons sugar
6 cups white bread flour

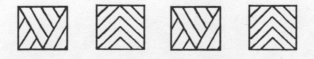

SECOND PROOF AND BAKING

Save and refrigerate 1 cup of culture from the first proof before proceeding.

1. Measure the culture into a large mixing bowl. Melt the butter over moderate heat (or melt in the microwave). Add the milk to the butter and warm briefly (to 75° to 85°), add the salt and sugar, and stir until dissolved. Add this mixture to the culture and mix well.

2. Add the flour, 1 cup at a time, stirring until the dough is too stiff to mix by hand. Turn onto a floured board and knead in the remaining flour until the dough is smooth and satiny. Divide the dough in half and form 2 balls.

3. Pat each ball into a 1-inch-thick oval and form loaves by rolling the ovals up from the long side, pinching the seam together as you roll the dough to form the loaf.

4. Place in loaf pans and proof, covered, at 85° for $1^{1}/_{2}$ to 3 hours. When the dough rises 1 to 2 inches above the edges of the pan, it is ready to bake.

5. Preheat the oven to 375°. Bake for 10 minutes, then reduce the heat to 350° and bake an additional 45 minutes.

6. Remove the loaves from the oven, and brush the tops lightly with melted butter. Turn the loaves out of the pans and cool on a wire rack.

Light Swedish Limpa

Makes 2 loaves

Limpa is a rye bread flavored with brown sugar or molasses. This one uses brown sugar, but many of the Austrian limpas use both. The orange zest is an absolute requirement to complement the light rye flavor. Use a coarse grater to produce substantial strips and chunks of the orange zest. I bake this bread in loaf pans, but it can be formed into French loaves.

> 4 cups culture from the first proof (page 37)
>
> 2 tablespoons butter
>
> 1 cup water
>
> 2 teaspoons salt
>
> $^1/_2$ cup firmly packed brown sugar
>
> Grated zest of 1 orange
>
> 1 tablespoon caraway seeds
>
> 2 tablespoons fennel seeds
>
> 1 cup rye flour
>
> 5 cups white bread flour

SECOND PROOF AND BAKING

1. Measure the culture into a large mixing bowl. Melt the butter over moderate heat. Add the water to the butter and warm (to 75° to 85°). Add the salt, brown sugar, orange zest, caraway seeds, and fennel seeds and stir. Add this mixture to the culture and mix well.

2. Add the rye flour and mix well. Add the white flour, 1 cup at a time, stirring until it is too stiff to mix by hand. Turn onto a floured board and knead in the remaining flour until the dough is smooth and satiny.

3. Divide dough in half and form 2 balls.

4. Pat each ball into a 1-inch-thick oval and form loaves by rolling the ovals from the long side, pinching the seam together as you roll the dough, to form the loaf.

5. Place in loaf pans and proof at 85°F for $1^1/_2$ to 3 hours. When dough rises 1 to 2 inches above the edges of the pan, it is ready to bake.

6. Preheat oven to 375°. Bake for 50 to 55 minutes.

7. Remove loaves from pans and cool on wire racks.

Tanya's Peasant Black Bread

Makes 1 loaf

My friend Tanya says this recipe really doesn't duplicate the bread of her native Russia, and I may yet have to go there to discover the secret of their ingredients. The combination of coriander and molasses complements the sourdough flavor, so don't leave either out.

> 2 cups culture from the first proof (page 37)
>
> 1/2 cup milk
>
> 2 tablespoons dark molasses
>
> 2 tablespoons vegetable oil
>
> 2 tablespoons sugar
>
> 1 teaspoon salt
>
> 1 teaspoon ground coriander
>
> 1 cup rye flour
>
> 1 cup whole wheat flour
>
> 1 1/2 cups white bread flour

SECOND PROOF AND BAKING

1. Measure the culture into a large mixing bowl. Warm the milk (to 75° to 85°).

2. Add the molasses, oil, sugar, salt, and coriander to the warm milk, mix briefly, and add to the culture.

3. Add the rye flour and mix well. Add the whole wheat flour and mix well. Add the white flour, stirring until it is too stiff to mix by hand.

4. Turn onto a floured board and knead in the remaining flour until the dough is smooth and satiny.

5. Form an oval loaf by flattening the dough to a 1 1/2-inch-thick oval and folding it once in half. Pinch the seam together.

6. Place on a baking sheet, seam side down, covered, and proof at 85° for 2 to 3 hours or until about doubled in bulk.

7. Bake at 375°F. for 45 to 50 minutes. Cool on a wire rack.

French Bread

Makes 2 loaves

Sourdough breads fell out of favor in French cities after the turn of the century, when commercial yeast became available. Recently, however, sourdoughs are back in vogue and, once again, prevail in the smaller bakeries of France. Much has been written about the difficulties of emulating the French bakery, with its steam ovens and special brick. Fear not! You can produce an authentic French loaf in your own kitchen with your own steam. This really works!

2 cups culture from the first proof (page 37)
1 teaspoon salt
¹/₂ cup warm water
4 cups white bread flour
2 tablespoons white cornmeal

SECOND PROOF AND BAKING

1. Measure the culture into a large mixing bowl. Add salt and water to the culture and mix well.

2. Add the flour 1 cup at a time, stirring until it is too stiff to mix by hand. Turn onto a floured board and knead in the remaining flour until the dough is smooth and satiny.

3. Divide into 2 equal portions and form oval, elongate loaves by flattening the dough to 1¹/₂-inch-thick ovals and folding them in half once. Pinch seams.

4. Sprinkle the cornmeal on a baking sheet and place the loaves on the sheet, seam side down. Proof at 85° for 2 hours, or until about doubled in bulk.

5. Preheat the oven to 375°. Make diagonal slashes in tops of the loaves with a razor blade.

6. When you place the loaves in the oven, spray them and the oven immediately with water from a fine mister. Repeat this spraying 3 additional times at 5-minute intervals. If the oven light is hot, avoid spraying it.

7. Continue baking for 30 to 40 minutes or until brown.

8. Remove loaves from baking sheet and cool on wire racks.

Whole Wheat Bread

Makes 2 loaves

This is Bob Linville's favorite and for good reason. It is a winner in both flavor and texture. He uses our fast Russian culture to leaven this moderately heavy dough.

> **4 cups culture from the first proof (page 37)**
>
> **2 teaspoons salt**
>
> **2 tablespoons sugar**
>
> **1 cup warm milk**
>
> **2 tablespoons butter, melted**
>
> **3 cups whole wheat flour**
>
> **3 cups white bread flour**

SECOND PROOF AND BAKING

1. Measure the culture into a large mixing bowl. Add the salt, sugar, milk, and melted butter to the culture and mix well.

2. Add the whole wheat flour and mix well. Add the white flour, 1 cup at a time, stirring until it is too stiff to mix by hand. Turn onto a floured board and knead in the remaining flour until the dough is smooth and satiny.

3. Divide into 2 equal portions.

4. Form loaves by flattening the dough to 1-inch-thick ovals and rolling the ovals from the long side, pinching the seams together.

5. Place loaves on baking sheets and proof, covered, at 85°, for 2 to 3 hours, or until doubled in bulk.

6. Preheat the oven to 375°. Make diagonal slashes in the tops of loaves.

7. Bake for 40 to 45 minutes.

8. Remove loaves from baking sheets and cool on wire racks.

Sour Cream Rye Bread

Makes 2 loaves

This is a heavy rye dough that will rise slowly, so consider using gluten flour (see page 31) if the dough doesn't rise enough the first time you make it. With an aggressive Russian culture you probably won't need it.

4 cups culture from the first proof (page 37)
2 teaspoons salt
4 teaspoons sugar
2 tablespoons oil
1 cup sour cream
2 tablespoons caraway seeds
4 cups rye flour
2 cups white bread flour

SECOND PROOF AND BAKING

1. Measure the culture into a large mixing bowl. Add salt, sugar, oil, sour cream, and caraway seeds to the culture and mix well.

2. Add the rye flour and mix. Add the white flour, stirring until it is too stiff to mix by hand. Turn onto a floured board and knead in remaining flour until the dough is smooth and satiny.

3. Divide dough into 2 equal balls.

4. Flatten with your hand or a rolling pin to form ovals 1^1/$_2$ inches thick. Make oval loaves by folding the ovals in the middle and pinching the edges together. Place on a baking sheet, seams down.

5. Proof, covered, at 85° for 2 to 3 hours, or until doubled in bulk.

6. Preheat oven to 375°. Make crisscross slashes in tops of loaves.

7. Bake for 55 minutes. Remove loaves from baking sheet and cool on wire racks.

Date Bread

Makes 1 loaf

Dates are the fruit of the desert. This recipe has them in a loaf leavened by wild yeast. It is a heavy dough and cannot be hurried.

> **2 cups culture from the first proof (page 37)**
> **¹/₂ cup water**
> **2 tablespoons oil**
> **1 cup chopped dates**
> **1 cup chopped nuts**
> **¹/₄ cup sugar**
> **1 teaspoon salt**
> **3 cups white bread flour**

Second Proof and Baking

1. Measure the culture into a large mixing bowl. Add water, oil, dates, nuts, sugar, and salt to the culture and mix well.

2. Add flour to the culture and mix well. You will probably have to knead in the last cup.

3. Form a loaf and place in a loaf pan. Proof, covered, at 85° for 2 to 3 hours.

4. Preheat oven to 375°. Bake for 55 to 60 minutes. Turn out of the pan and cool on a wire rack.

Dinner Rolls

Makes 8 to 20 rolls

This recipe makes either 8 to 12 Parker House rolls or 16 to 20 dinner rolls. For the latter, use 3 cups of culture and 4 cups of flour. This is one recipe in which I use all-purpose flour to produce a lighter texture. The rolls can be glazed with poppy or sesame seeds, if you like. Brush the tops with beaten egg and sprinkle on the seeds before baking.

> **2 cups culture from the first proof (page 37)**
> **3 tablespoons butter, melted**
> **1 egg, beaten**
> **$1/2$ cup milk**
> **1 tablespoon sugar**
> **1 teaspoon salt**
> **3 cups white all-purpose flour**

SECOND PROOF AND BAKING

1. Measure the culture into a large mixing bowl. Add 2 tablespoons of the melted butter, the egg, milk, sugar, and salt to the culture and mix briefly.

2. Add the flour, 1 cup at a time, stirring until it is too stiff to mix by hand. Turn onto a floured board and knead in remaining flour until dough is satiny.

3. For Parker House rolls, roll dough out to a thickness of $1/2$ inch. Cut rounds with a 3-inch cookie cutter or an empty 15-ounce can with the top and bottom removed. Crease with a knife slightly off the middle. Brush rounds lightly, using about 1 tablespoon melted butter, and fold the larger part over the smaller. Place on a baking sheet and proof, covered, at 85° for 1 hour.

   For dinner rolls, form dough into 16 to 20 small balls and place them side by side in an 8-inch square baking pan. Proof, covered, at 85° until they rise above the sides of the pan.

4. Preheat oven to 375°. Bake for 20 to 25 minutes, or until brown. Remove rolls from pan and cool on a wire rack.

Finnish Rye Bread

Makes 2 loaves

The addition of brown sugar imparts a golden brown color and enhances the flavor of this moderately heavy rye bread. It may rise slowly. It is a favorite in Scandinavia, where long winters allow plenty of time for proofing.

4 cups culture from the first proof (page 37)

1 cup milk

1 tablespoon salt

6 tablespoons firmly packed dark brown sugar

2 tablespoons butter, melted

3 cups rye flour

3 cups white bread flour

SECOND PROOF AND BAKING

1. Measure the culture into a large mixing bowl. Add milk, salt, brown sugar, and melted butter to the culture and mix well.

2. Add the rye flour and mix. Add the white flour, 1 cup at a time, stirring until it is too stiff to mix by hand. Turn onto a floured board and knead in remaining flour until dough is satiny.

3. Form into 2 equal balls.

4. Pat or roll balls into flat rounds about 1½ inches thick. Form round loaves by folding in the middle, and seal edges by pinching. Place on a baking sheet.

5. Proof, covered, at 85° for 3 to 4 hours, or until doubled in bulk.

6. Preheat oven to 375°. Make crisscross slashes in tops of loaves.

7. Bake for 55 to 60 minutes. Remove loaves from baking sheet and cool on wire racks.

Raisin Rye Bread

Makes 2 loaves

This is an excellent bread for breakfast toast. For variety, substitute whole wheat flour for rye flour and use 2 tablespoons of brown sugar instead of the granulated sugar.

4 cups culture from the first proof (page 37)

1 cup water

2 teaspoons salt

1 tablespoon sugar

1 tablespoon oil

2 cups raisins, plumped (see Note)

2 cups rye flour

4 cups white bread flour

GLAZE
1 egg, beaten
1 tablespoon milk

SECOND PROOF AND BAKING

1. Measure the culture into a large mixing bowl. Add water, salt, sugar, oil, and raisins to the culture and mix well.

2. Add the rye flour and mix. Add the white flour, 1 cup at a time, stirring until it is too stiff to mix by hand. Turn onto a floured board and knead in remaining flour until dough is satiny.

3. Form into 2 equal balls. Pat or roll into flat ovals 1½ inches thick, and form loaves by folding in the middle. Seal edges by pinching and place seam side down on a baking sheet.

4. Proof, covered, at 85° for 2 to 3 hours, or until doubled in bulk.

5. Preheat oven to 375°. Combine ingredients for glaze and brush on loaves.

6. Bake for 55 to 60 minutes. Remove loaves from baking sheet and cool on wire racks.

NOTE: To plump raisins, soak them in water to cover for 30 minutes, or place in water to cover and microwave on high for 2 minutes. Cool before adding to culture.

Pumpernickel Rye Bread

Makes 3 loaves

Pumpernickel is a coarsely ground rye grain with poor or no gluten; it therefore does not rise especially well. It does produce a moist, dark bread ideal for buffets. I have used Vital gluten flour in this recipe with good results.

> **4 cups culture from the first proof (page 37)**
> **1 cup milk**
> **2 teaspoons salt**
> **4 teaspoons sugar**
> **2 tablespoons oil**
> **1 tablespoon caraway seeds**
> **3 cups coarse pumpernickel flour**
> **3 cups white bread flour**

SECOND PROOF AND BAKING

1. Measure the culture into a large mixing bowl. Add milk, salt, sugar, oil, and caraway seeds to the culture and mix.

2. Add the pumpernickel flour and mix well. Add the white flour, 1 cup at a time, stirring until it is too stiff to mix by hand. Turn onto a floured board and knead in remaining flour until dough is satiny.

3. Form 3 equal balls and flatten into 2-inch-thick rounds.

4. Fold over once to form oval loaves. Pinch seams to seal.

5. Place on a baking sheet, seam side down, and proof, covered, at 85° for 2 to 3 hours, or until doubled in bulk.

6. Preheat oven to 400°. Make crisscross slashes in tops of loaves.

7. Bake for 55 to 60 minutes. Brush loaves with melted butter, remove from baking sheet, and cool on wire racks.

Egg Braid

Makes 2 loaves

I enjoy making braided bread, and the finished product is attractive. I start the braid at one end and work to the other end, but you may find it easier to start in the middle and braid in both directions.

4 cups culture from the first proof (page 37)

2 tablespoons butter

1 cup milk

2 teaspoons salt

2 tablespoons sugar

2 eggs, beaten

6 cups white bread flour

GLAZE
1 egg, beaten

Sesame seeds

SECOND PROOF AND BAKING

1. Measure the culture into a large mixing bowl. Melt the butter over moderate heat, add the milk, and warm (to 75° to 85°). (Or using the microwave oven, melt and warm the butter and milk in one step.) Add the salt and sugar and stir until dissolved. Add this mixture to the culture and mix well.

2. Add the eggs and mix.

3. Add the flour, 1 cup at a time, stirring until it is too stiff to mix by hand. Turn onto a floured board and knead in remaining flour until dough is satiny.

4. Divide dough in half and form 2 balls.

5. Divide each ball into 3 equal portions and roll each to form 3 "ropes" about 18 inches long and $^1/_2$ to 1 inch in diameter.

6. Form a braid from each group of three.

7. Place on baking sheets and proof, covered, at 85° for 1 to 2 hours, or until doubled in bulk.

8. Preheat oven to 375°. Brush the tops of the loaves with beaten egg and sprinkle with sesame seeds.

9. Bake for 35 to 40 minutes. Remove loaves from baking sheets and cool on wire racks.

BRAIDING DOUGH

This is an alternative method for making strands of dough for braiding:

1. Form into a "log" 3 inches in diameter.

2. Roll dough lengthwise to a rectangle 1/2 inch thick, 9 inches wide, and 18 inches long. With a pizza cutter, cut 6 strips lengthwise (each 1 1/2 inches wide).

3. Fold each strip over to make a rounder strip, and crimp edges together.

4. Using 3 strips for each braided loaf:

   • Lay one strand on counter or board. Place the other two strands over it so that they cross in the middle.

   • Starting at the center, alternately cross the outside strands over the one in the center.

   • As you work, gently pull to taper the ends.

   • When you reach the end, rotate the whole piece 180° and braid the other side.

   • Pinch the ends together and tuck them under the braid to finish.

Dark Pumpernickel Bread

Makes 2 loaves

This is a heavy, moist, dark bread found throughout Europe. It rises slowly and requires patience for the final proof. It is worth the wait. Pumpernickel is a coarse rye meal with bran particles. The average supermarket doesn't stock it; where I live, I have to search for it in specialty food stores.

> **4 cups culture from the first proof (page 37)**
>
> **2 teaspoons salt**
>
> **4 teaspoons sugar**
>
> **1 cup milk**
>
> **2 tablespoons oil**
>
> **1 tablespoon caraway seeds**
>
> **1/2 cup white bread flour**
>
> **2 cups whole wheat flour**
>
> **3 cups coarse pumpernickel flour**

SECOND PROOF AND BAKING

1. Measure the culture into a large mixing bowl. Add salt, sugar, milk, oil, and caraway seeds to the culture and mix well.

2. Combine the flours in a separate bowl and mix. Add the flour mixture, 1 cup at a time, stirring until it is too stiff to mix by hand. Turn onto a floured board and knead in remaining flour until dough is satiny.

3. Divide dough into 2 equal balls.

4. Flatten by hand or with a rolling pin and form ovals 1 1/2 inches thick. Make oval loaves by folding in the middle and pinching the edges together. Place on a baking sheet, seam side down.

5. Proof, covered, at 85° for 2 to 3 hours, or until doubled in bulk.

6. Preheat oven to 375°. Make crisscross slashes in tops of loaves.

7. Bake for 55 to 60 minutes. Remove loaves from baking sheet and cool on wire racks.

Challah

Makes 1 loaf

This is a Hebrew Sabbath bread, dating back to biblical times.

4 cups culture from the first proof (page 37)

3 tablespoons butter

1 cup milk

2 teaspoons salt

3 tablespoons sugar

2 eggs, beaten

6 cups white bread flour

GLAZE

1 egg, beaten

1 tablespoon sesame seeds

SECOND PROOF AND BAKING

1. Measure the culture into a large mixing bowl. Melt the butter over moderate heat, add the milk to the butter, and warm (to 75° to 85°). (Or, using the microwave oven, melt and warm the butter and milk in one step.) Add the salt, sugar, and eggs and stir until dissolved. Add this mixture to the culture and mix well.

2. Add the flour, 1 cup at a time, stirring until it is too stiff to mix by hand. Turn onto a floured board and knead in remaining flour until dough is satiny.

3. Divide the dough into 4 equal balls.

4. Roll each ball into a rope about 18 to 20 inches long and 1 inch in diameter.

5. Pinch the four ropes together at one end and braid by bringing the rope on the right over the one next to it, under the third one and over the last one. Repeat, always starting with the rope on the right until the braid is complete. Pinch the ends together.

6. Place on a baking sheet and proof, covered, at 85° for 1 to 2 hours, or until about doubled in bulk.

7. Preheat oven to 375°. Brush the loaf with beaten egg and sprinkle with sesame seeds. Bake for 35 minutes. Remove from baking sheet and cool on a wire rack.

Cheese Bread

Makes 1 loaf

Cheese breads are a pleasant variation on traditional Middle Eastern flatbreads. This one is lightly leavened.

2 cups culture from the first proof (page 37)

1 teaspoon salt

2 teaspoons sugar

$1/2$ cup water

2 tablespoons oil

3 cups white bread flour

8 ounces cream cheese, softened

GLAZE
1 egg, beaten
Sesame seeds

SECOND PROOF AND BAKING

1. Measure the culture into a large mixing bowl. Add salt, sugar, water, and oil to the culture and mix well.

2. Add the flour, 1 cup at a time, stirring until it is too stiff to mix by hand. Turn out on a floured board and knead in remaining flour until dough is satiny.

3. Flatten by hand or with a rolling pin into a rectangle $1/2$ inch thick.

4. Spread the cheese over the dough rectangle, leaving a 1-inch margin on all sides.

5. Roll up from the long side and pinch the ends to seal, forming an oval elongate loaf.

6. Place on a baking sheet.

7. Proof, covered, at 85° for 1 to 2 hours, or until about doubled in bulk. Then brush the top with beaten egg and sprinkle with sesame seeds.

8. Preheat oven to 375°. Bake 40 to 45 minutes. Remove from baking sheet and cool on a wire rack.

Onion Olive Bread

Makes 1 loaf

This is a delicious bread originally from Greece and Cyprus.

2 cups culture from the first proof (page 37)
1 onion, finely chopped
1 tablespoon olive oil
1 cup chopped black olives
1 teaspoon salt
2¹/₂ cups white bread flour

SECOND PROOF AND BAKING

1. Measure the culture into a large mixing bowl. Sauté onion in the olive oil until just transparent. Combine olives with onions and cool.

2. Add salt to the culture and mix well.

3. Add the flour to the culture, stirring, until it is too stiff to mix by hand. Turn onto a floured board and knead in remaining flour until dough is satiny.

4. Flatten by hand or with a rolling pin into a rectangle about ¹/₂ inch thick.

5. Spread onion and olive mixture over surface of dough, leaving a 1-inch margin on all sides.

6. Roll up from the long side into a loaf, and pinch ends to seal.

7. Place on a baking sheet and proof, covered, at 85° for 1 hour, or until doubled in bulk.

8. Make several diagonal slashes in top of loaf with a razor blade.

9. Preheat oven to 375°. Brush top with oil and bake for 45 to 50 minutes. Remove loaf from baking sheet and cool on a wire rack.

Malt Beer Bread

Makes 2 loaves

Experiment with different beers in this bread. I've used dark beers from Germany and Scandinavia to complement the rye flavor, but many of the local beers now produced by American microbreweries are just as good.

4 cups culture from the first proof (page 37)

2 teaspoons salt

2 tablespoons sugar

1 cup malt beer

2 tablespoons butter, melted

3 cups rye flour

3 cups white bread flour

SECOND PROOF AND BAKING

1. Measure the culture into a large mixing bowl. Add the salt, sugar, and beer to the melted butter and stir until dissolved. Add this mixture to the culture and mix well.

2. Add the rye flour and mix. Add the white flour, 1 cup at a time, stirring until it is too stiff to mix by hand. Turn onto a floured board and knead in remaining flour until dough is satiny.

3. Divide dough in half and form 2 balls. Form into loaves.

4. Place in loaf pans and proof, covered, at 85° for 1 1/2 to 3 hours. When dough rises 1 to 2 inches above edges of pans, it is ready to bake.

5. Preheat oven to 375°. Bake for 50 to 55 minutes.

6. Remove loaves from pans and cool on wire racks.

Caraway Rye Bread

Makes 2 loaves

Few ingredients make a better combination than caraway and rye. Although many of these recipes utilize caraway, this one particularly enhances the two flavors.

> **4 cups culture from the first proof (page 37)**
>
> **1 cup water**
>
> **2 tablespoons butter, melted**
>
> **2 teaspoons salt**
>
> **³/₄ cup dark molasses**
>
> **2 tablespoons caraway seeds**
>
> **2 cups light rye flour**
>
> **4 cups white bread flour**

SECOND PROOF AND BAKING

1. Measure the culture into a large mixing bowl. Add water, butter, salt, molasses, and caraway seeds to the culture and mix.

2. Add the rye flour and mix. Add the white flour, 1 cup at a time, stirring until it is too stiff to mix by hand. Turn onto a floured board and knead in remaining flour until dough is satiny.

3. Form 2 equal balls.

4. Press into flat ovals 1 inch thick and roll into loaves. Pinch seams together.

5. Place in loaf pans and proof, covered, at 85° for 2 to 3 hours, or until doubled in bulk.

6. Preheat oven to 400°. Bake for 55 minutes. Remove loaves from pans and cool on wire racks.

German Rye Bread

Makes 3 loaves

For those who prefer a more subtle and delicate rye flavor, a single cup of rye flour is ideal. This bread rises well and is a favorite in southern Austria as well as in Germany.

4 cups culture from the first proof (page 37)

1 cup milk

2 teaspoons salt

2 tablespoons molasses

2 tablespoons oil

1 cup rye flour

5 cups white bread flour

GLAZE
1 egg, beaten
Caraway seeds

SECOND PROOF AND BAKING

1. Measure the culture into a large mixing bowl. Add milk, salt, molasses, and oil to the culture and mix well.

2. Add the rye flour and mix. Add the white flour, 1 cup at a time, stirring until it is too stiff to mix. Turn onto a floured board and knead in remaining flour until dough is satiny.

3. Divide the dough into 3 equal balls.

4. Form into loaves and place on baking sheets or in loaf pans.

5. Proof, covered, at 85° for 2 to 3 hours, or until doubled in bulk.

6. Preheat oven to 375°. Brush with beaten egg and sprinkle with caraway seeds. Make diagonal slashes on loaves in pans or crisscross slashes on oval loaves.

7. Bake for 50 to 60 minutes. Remove loaves from pans and cool on wire racks.

Austrian Wheat Rye Bread

Makes 2 loaves

The combination of white and rye flours produces a moderate rye flavor. The bread rises well but will result in a somewhat heavier loaf. The addition of anise and caraway imparts the typical flavor so characteristic of European rye bread.

> **4 cups culture from the first proof (page 37)**
>
> **1 cup milk**
>
> **2 teaspoons salt**
>
> **2 tablespoons sugar**
>
> **1 tablespoon caraway seeds**
>
> **1 teaspoon anise seed**
>
> **1 teaspoon ground cumin**
>
> **2 cups rye flour**
>
> **4 cups white bread flour**

SECOND PROOF AND BAKING

1. Measure the culture into a large mixing bowl. Add the milk, salt, sugar, caraway seeds, anise seed, and cumin to the culture and mix well.

2. Add rye flour and mix well. Add the white flour, 1 cup at a time, stirring until it is too stiff to mix by hand. Turn onto a floured board and knead in remaining flour until dough is satiny.

3. Divide dough into 2 equal balls.

4. Flatten balls to 1-inch-thick rounds, fold in half to form oval loaves, and pinch seams. Place on a baking sheet.

5. Proof, covered, at 85° for 2 to 3 hours, or until about doubled in bulk.

6. Preheat oven to 400°. Make crisscross slashes in tops of loaves.

7. Bake for 45 to 60 minutes (depending on size of loaves). Remove loaves from baking sheet and cool on wire racks.

Baguettes

Makes 3 loaves

This chewy French loaf should be made as long as your oven (or baking sheet) will permit. The recipe says 18 inches, but if your oven is bigger, stretch the roll as long as possible. Several baguette molds are available that help form the characteristic shape of this loaf. Wilton supplies one made of aluminum that is 17 inches by 9 inches and holds 3 baguettes. It is a good idea to put a baking sheet under the mold to make it easier to maneuver in and out of the oven.

4 cups culture from the first proof (page 37)

2 tablespoons butter

1 cup milk

2 teaspoons salt

2 tablespoons sugar

6 cups white bread flour

GLAZE
2 eggs, beaten

SECOND PROOF AND BAKING

1. Measure the culture into a large mixing bowl. Melt the butter over moderate heat, add the milk to the butter and warm (to 75° to 85°). Add the salt and sugar and stir until dissolved. Add this mixture to the culture and mix well.

2. Add the flour, 1 cup at a time, stirring until it is too stiff to mix by hand. Turn onto a floured board and knead in remaining flour until dough is satiny.

3. Divide dough in thirds and form 3 balls. Use a rolling pin to roll out each ball into a rectangle.

4. Roll each rectangle from the long side to form an elongate loaf. The loaf should be about 18 inches long and $1^1/2$ inches in diameter.

5. Place on baking sheets or in a baguette mold and proof, covered, at 85° for 1 to 2 hours, or until about doubled in bulk.

6. Brush with beaten egg.

7. Preheat oven to 375°. Make diagonal slashes across tops of loaves.

8. Bake for 35 minutes.

9. Remove from baking sheets and cool on wire racks.

Bread Ring

Makes 1 ring

Bread rings and braided pastries are common in the Middle East; this recipe produces a fine, light, and delicious loaf. When you want to experiment, replace 1 cup of the white flour with 1 cup of Kamut or spelt.

> **2 cups culture from the first proof (page 37)**
> **1 teaspoon salt**
> **1 tablespoon sugar**
> **¹/₂ cup water**
> **2 tablespoons oil**
> **3 cups white bread flour**
> **Sesame seeds**

SECOND PROOF AND BAKING

1. Measure the culture into a large mixing bowl. Add salt, sugar, water, and oil to the culture and mix.

2. Add the flour to the culture, 1 cup at a time, stirring until it is too stiff to mix by hand. Turn onto a floured board and knead in remaining flour until dough is satiny.

3. Flatten by hand or with a rolling pin into a large oval. Roll into a tight rope. Continue rolling back and forth until it is approximately 20 to 24 inches long. Form into a ring by joining the ends.

4. Place on a baking sheet. Cover and proof at 85° for 1 to 2 hours.

5. Preheat oven to 375°. Brush top with water, and sprinkle with sesame seeds.

6. Bake for 35 to 40 minutes. Remove ring from baking sheet and cool on a wire rack.

White French Bread

Makes 2 loaves

This is a conventional loaf bread, delicious but not the well-known French loaf.

4 cups culture from the first proof (page 37)
2 eggs, beaten
1 teaspoon salt
2 teaspoons sugar
1/2 cup milk
2 tablespoons butter, melted
6 cups white bread flour

GLAZE
1/4 cup milk
Poppy seeds

SECOND PROOF AND BAKING

1. Measure the culture into a large mixing bowl. Add beaten eggs, salt, sugar, milk, and melted butter to the culture and mix.

2. Add the flour, 1 cup at a time, stirring until it is too stiff to mix by hand. Turn onto a floured board and knead in remaining flour until dough is satiny.

3. Form 2 balls.

4. Pat to 1½-inch-thick rounds and form oblong loaves.

5. Place in loaf pans and proof, covered, at 85° for 2 hours, or until bread has risen above the edges of the pans to the desired volume.

6. Preheat oven to 400°. Brush tops of loaves with milk and sprinkle with poppy seeds.

7. Bake 45 to 55 minutes. Remove loaves from pans and cool on wire racks.

Cheese-Onion Bread

Makes 2 loaves

Adding freshly chopped onion to this cheese bread yields a truly delicious loaf. The onion adds liquid, which sometimes requires the addition of more flour. Test a loaf with a digital thermometer when it is removed from the oven. The center should be 190°. Toast the slices for the "right out of the oven" aroma. This dough can also be braided, if you prefer.

> **4 cups culture from the first proof (page 37)**
>
> **2 tablespoons butter**
>
> **1 cup milk**
>
> **2 teaspoons salt**
>
> **2 tablespoons sugar**
>
> **2 cups grated Cheddar cheese (not packed)**
>
> **1 cup finely chopped onion**
>
> **6 cups white bread flour**

SECOND PROOF AND BAKING

1. Measure the culture into a large mixing bowl. Melt the butter over moderate heat, add the milk to the butter, and warm (to 75° to 85°). Add the salt, sugar, loosely grated cheese, and onion and stir. Add this mixture to the culture and mix well.

2. Add the flour, 1 cup at a time, stirring until it is too stiff to mix by hand. Turn onto a floured board and knead in remaining flour until dough is satiny.

3. Divide dough in half and form 2 balls.

4. Pat each ball into a 1-inch-thick oval and form loaves by rolling from the long side, pinching the seam together as you roll the dough to form the loaf.

5. Place in loaf pans and proof, covered, at 85° for 1½ to 3 hours. This is a moist loaf, and it may take longer to rise. When dough rises 1 to 2 inches above the rims of the pans, it is ready to bake.

6. Preheat oven to 375°. Bake for 50 to 55 minutes.

7. Remove loaves from pans and cool on wire racks.

Onion Bread

Makes 2 loaves

Onions and rye flour provide a pleasing flavor combination. This recipe uses chopped onions lightly sautéed in olive oil. Raw chopped onions work equally well and dried onion can also be used. Raw onions will increase the liquid.

4 cups culture from the first proof (page 37)
1 cup chopped onions
1 tablespoon olive oil
2 tablespoons butter
1/2 cup water
2 teaspoons salt
4 cups rye flour
2 cups white bread flour

SECOND PROOF AND BAKING

1. Measure the culture into a large mixing bowl. Sauté onions in olive oil.

2. Melt the butter over moderate heat, add the water to the butter and warm (to 75° to 85°). Add the salt and stir until dissolved. Add the onions. Add this mixture to the culture and mix well.

3. Add the rye flour and mix well. Add the white flour, 1 cup at a time, stirring until it is too stiff to mix by hand. Turn onto a floured board and knead in remaining flour until dough is satiny.

4. Divide dough in half and form 2 balls.

5. Shape into 2 elongate loaves.

6. Place on baking sheets and proof, covered, at 85° for 1 to 2 hours, or until about doubled in bulk.

7. Preheat oven to 375°. Make diagonal slashes in tops of loaves.

8. Bake for 50 to 55 minutes.

9. Remove loaves from baking sheets and cool on wire racks.

Potato Bread

Makes 2 loaves

Prepared instant mashed potatoes (1 cup) may be substituted for the boiled potatoes if desired. The addition of either provides a distinctive flavor and texture to this hearty white bread. Many of the older sourdough bakers fed their "starters" with boiled potatoes, but the addition here is primarily for flavor. Naturally, I use my home-grown Idaho spuds.

> 4 cups culture from the first proof (page 37)
> 2 tablespoons butter
> 1 cup milk
> 2 teaspoons salt
> 2 medium potatoes, boiled and mashed
> 6 cups white bread flour

SECOND PROOF AND BAKING

1. Measure the culture into a large mixing bowl. Melt the butter over moderate heat, add the milk to the butter, and warm (to 75° to 85°). Add the salt and mashed potatoes and stir well. Add this mixture to the culture and mix well.

2. Add the flour, 1 cup at a time, stirring until it is too stiff to mix by hand. Turn onto a floured board and knead in remaining flour until dough is satiny.

3. Divide dough in half and form 2 balls.

4. Shape into oblong loaves.

5. Place on baking sheets and proof, covered, at 85° for 1 to 2 hours, or until about doubled in bulk.

6. Preheat oven to 375°. Bake for 50 to 55 minutes.

7. Remove loaves from baking sheets and cool on wire racks.

Rosemary Bread

Makes 1 loaf

This Italian bread is baked especially for Easter. Fresh rosemary can be lightly browned in olive oil to flavor the oil. (Then discard the rosemary.) This recipe, however, uses dry rosemary directly in the dough mixture.

> **2 cups culture from the first proof (page 37)**
> **¹/₂ cup warm milk**
> **¹/₄ cup olive oil**
> **1 teaspoon salt**
> **1 tablespoon sugar**
> **1 teaspoon dry rosemary, ground**
> **¹/₂ cup raisins**
> **2 eggs, beaten**
> **3 cups white bread flour**
> **1 egg, beaten**

SECOND PROOF AND BAKING

1. Measure the culture into a large mixing bowl. Add the milk, olive oil, salt, sugar, rosemary, raisins, and 2 beaten eggs to the culture and mix well.

2. Add the flour, 1 cup at a time, stirring until it is too stiff to mix by hand. Turn onto a floured board and knead in remaining flour until dough is satiny.

3. Form an oval or round loaf.

4. Place on a baking sheet and proof, covered, for 1 to 2 hours, or until about doubled in bulk.

5. Preheat oven to 350°. Make crisscross slash in top of loaf.

6. Brush with the remaining beaten egg.

7. Bake for 45 minutes.

8. Remove loaf from baking sheet and cool on a wire rack.

Graham and Cracked-Wheat Bread

Makes 2 loaves

Cracked wheat is produced by a cutting process instead of by grinding. It can be used raw, as in this recipe, or cooked. If cooked, it is usually presoaked for several hours and then simmered for about 1 hour in 2 cups of water for every cup of cracked grain.

> **4 cups culture from the first proof (page 37)**
> **2 tablespoons butter**
> **1 cup milk**
> **2 teaspoons salt**
> **$1/2$ cup molasses**
> **2 tablespoons sugar**
> **$1/4$ cup cracked wheat**
> **$1^1/2$ cups graham flour**
> **5 cups white bread flour**

SECOND PROOF AND BAKING

1. Measure the culture into a large mixing bowl. Melt the butter over moderate heat, add the milk to the butter and warm (to 75° to 85°). (Or mix the butter and milk together and warm them in a microwave oven.) Add the salt, molasses, and sugar and stir until dissolved. Add this mixture to the culture and mix well.

2. Add the cracked wheat and graham flour and mix well. Add the white flour, 1 cup at a time, stirring until it is too stiff to mix by hand. Then turn onto a floured board and knead in remaining flour until dough is satiny.

3. Divide dough in half and form 2 balls.

4. Form into loaves and place in loaf pans. Proof, covered, at 85° for $1^1/2$ to 3 hours. When dough rises 1 to 2 inches above the edges of the pans, it is ready to bake.

5. Preheat oven to 375°. Bake for 50 to 55 minutes.

6. Remove loaves from pans and cool on wire racks.

Oatmeal Bread

Makes 2 loaves

This recipe produces an interesting variation. It is somewhat rougher in texture but rises well. I have also used steel-cut oats in this recipe.

> **4 cups culture from the first proof (page 37)**
> **1/2 cup milk**
> **1 teaspoon salt**
> **2 tablespoons firmly packed brown sugar**
> **2 cups rolled oats**
> **4 cups white bread flour**

SECOND PROOF AND BAKING

1. Measure the culture into a large mixing bowl. Add the milk, salt, sugar, and rolled oats to the culture and mix well.

2. Add the flour, 1 cup at a time, stirring until it is too stiff to mix by hand. Turn onto a floured board and knead in the remaining flour until dough is satiny.

3. Divide dough in half and form 2 balls.

4. Pat each ball into a 1-inch-thick oval and form loaves by rolling from the long side, pinching the seam together as you roll the dough to form the loaf.

5. Place in loaf pans and proof, covered, at 85° for 1 1/2 to 3 hours. When dough rises 1 to 2 inches above the edges of pans, it is ready to bake.

6. Preheat oven to 400°. Bake for 40 to 45 minutes.

7. Remove loaves from pans and cool on wire racks.

Sunflower Bread

Makes 2 loaves

Sunflower seeds can be used either raw, as in this recipe, or roasted. I much prefer raw seeds.

> **4 cups culture from the first proof (page 37)**
> **2 tablespoons butter**
> **1 cup milk**
> **2 teaspoons salt**
> **1/2 cup honey**
> **1 cup raw sunflower seeds**
> **3 cups whole wheat flour**
> **3 cups white bread flour**

SECOND PROOF AND BAKING

1. Measure the culture into a large mixing bowl. Melt the butter over moderate heat, add the milk to the butter, and warm (to 75° to 85°). Add the salt, honey, and sunflower seeds. Add this mixture to the culture and mix well.

2. Add the whole wheat flour and mix. Add the white flour, 1 cup at a time, stirring until it is too stiff to mix by hand. Then turn onto a floured board and knead in remaining flour until dough is satiny.

3. Divide dough in half and form 2 balls.

4. Pat each ball into a 1-inch-thick oval and form loaves by rolling from the long side, pinching the seam together as you roll the dough to form the loaf.

5. Place in loaf pans and proof, covered, at 85° for 1 1/2 to 3 hours. When dough rises 1 to 2 inches above the edges of the pan, it is ready to bake.

6. Preheat oven to 375°. Bake for 50 to 55 minutes.

7. Remove loaves from pans and cool on wire racks.

Walnut Bread

Makes 2 loaves

This recipe calls for chopped walnuts, but other nuts are equally suitable, and a mixture is even better. The ginger is essential for an extra-exquisite flavor.

4 cups culture from the first proof (page 37)

2 tablespoons butter

1 cup milk

2 teaspoons salt

1$^1/_2$ cups chopped walnuts

$^1/_2$ cup honey

$^1/_2$ teaspoon ground ginger

3 cups whole wheat flour

3 cups white bread flour

SECOND PROOF AND BAKING

1. Measure the culture into a large mixing bowl. Melt the butter over moderate heat, add the milk to the butter, and warm (to 75° to 85°). Add the salt, walnuts, honey, and ginger and stir. Add this mixture to the culture and mix well.

2. Add the whole wheat flour and mix well. Add the white flour, 1 cup at a time, stirring until it is too stiff to mix by hand. Turn onto a floured board and knead in remaining flour until dough is satiny.

3. Divide the dough in half and form 2 balls.

4. Pat each ball into a 1-inch-thick oval and form loaves by rolling from the long side, pinching the seam together as you roll the dough to form the loaf.

5. Place in loaf pans and proof, covered, at 85° for 1$^1/_2$ to 3 hours. When the dough rises 1 to 2 inches above the edges of the pans, it is ready to bake.

6. Preheat oven to 375°. Bake for 50 to 55 minutes.

7. Remove loaves from pans and cool on wire racks.

Herb Bread

Makes 2 loaves

This delightful loaf uses a mixture of thyme, oregano, and basil.

4 cups culture from the first proof (page 37)

2 tablespoons butter

1 cup milk

1 teaspoon salt

2 teaspoons sugar

1 teaspoon each dried thyme, oregano, and basil

6 cups white bread flour

SECOND PROOF AND BAKING

1. Measure the culture into a large mixing bowl. Melt the butter over moderate heat, add the milk to the butter, and warm (to 75° to 85°). Add the salt, sugar, thyme, oregano, and basil and stir. Add this mixture to the culture and mix well.

2. Add the flour, 1 cup at a time, stirring until it is too stiff to mix by hand. Turn onto a floured board and knead in remaining flour until dough is satiny.

3. Divide dough in half and form 2 balls.

4. Pat each ball into a 1-inch-thick oval and form loaves by rolling from the long side, pinching the seam together as you roll the dough to form the loaf.

5. Place on baking sheets and proof, covered, at 85° for 2 to 3 hours, or until about doubled in bulk.

6. Preheat oven to 375°. Bake for 55 to 60 minutes.

7. Remove loaves from baking sheets and cool on wire racks.

Cinnamon-Raisin Nut Bread

Makes 2 loaves

This is an excellent bread for morning toast. It may take as long as 3 hours to rise, so I make it well in advance.

> 4 cups culture from the first proof (page 37)
>
> 2 tablespoons butter, melted
>
> 1 cup warm milk (75° to 85°)
>
> 2 teaspoons salt
>
> 2 tablespoons sugar
>
> 1/4 cup ground cinnamon
>
> 1 cup chopped nuts
>
> 1 cup raisins
>
> 6 cups white bread flour
>
>
> **FILLING**
>
> 2 tablespoons ground cinnamon
>
> 1/2 cup sugar

SECOND PROOF AND BAKING

1. Measure the culture into a large mixing bowl. Stir in the melted butter, warm milk, salt, 2 tablespoons sugar, and cinnamon. Add the nuts and raisins and mix.

2. Add the flour, 1 cup at a time, stirring until the dough is too stiff to mix by hand. Turn onto a floured board and knead in remaining flour until the dough is smooth and satiny.

3. Divide dough in half and roll into rectangles the width of your loaf pan and about 1/2 inch thick.

4. To make the filling, mix 2 tablespoons cinnamon with 1/2 cup sugar. Sprinkle half of this mixture on each rectangle and roll up to form loaves.

5. Place in loaf pans and proof, covered, at 85° for up to 3 hours. When dough is about doubled in bulk, it is ready to bake.

6. Preheat oven to 350°. Bake for 55 minutes. Remove loaves from pans and cool on a wire rack.

Gingerbread

Makes 1 loaf

Baking soda helps to leaven this delicious bread; no additional proofing is required.

2 cups culture from the first proof (page 37)

2 tablespoons butter, melted

1 cup molasses

1 teaspoon ground cinnamon

1 teaspoon ground ginger

1 egg, beaten

2 tablespoons sugar

1 teaspoon salt

$^1/_2$ teaspoon baking soda

1 cup white bread flour

SECOND PROOF AND BAKING

1. Measure the culture into a large mixing bowl. Preheat oven to 350°. Add melted butter, molasses, cinnamon, ginger, egg, sugar, and salt to the culture and mix well.

2. Add baking soda to the flour and mix. Then add the flour to the culture and mix until smooth.

3. Pour into a greased and floured 10-inch square baking pan.

4. Bake for 55 to 60 minutes.

Austrian Christmas Bread

Makes 1 loaf

Sourdough may not come to mind when you think of Christmas breads, but remember all breads were made with sourdough in the beginning.

2 cups culture from the first proof (page 37)

¹/₂ cup milk

2 eggs, beaten

¹/₂ cup candied citron

¹/₂ cup raisins

1 tablespoon anise seed

1 teaspoon salt

3 tablespoons sugar

4 cups white bread flour

SECOND PROOF AND BAKING

1. Measure the culture into a large mixing bowl. Add milk, eggs, citron, raisins, anise seed, salt, and sugar to the culture and mix well.

2. Add the flour, 1 cup at a time, stirring until it is too stiff to mix by hand. Turn onto a floured board and knead in remaining flour until dough is satiny.

3. Form into a ball and make an oval loaf by flattening the ball to a 1¹/₂-inch-thick oval and folding once in half. Pinch seams together.

4. Place on a baking sheet, seam side down, and proof, covered, at 85° for 2 to 3 hours, or until about doubled in bulk.

5. Preheat oven to 350°. Bake for 55 to 60 minutes. Remove loaf from baking sheet and cool on a wire rack.

German Christmas Bread

Makes 1 loaf

Sweet yeast breads from Germany are known as stollens throughout Europe. You can substitute a mixture of candied fruits for the citron.

> **4 cups culture from the first proof (page 37)**
> **¹/₂ cup butter**
> **1 cup milk**
> **2 teaspoons salt**
> **¹/₂ cup raisins**
> **¹/₂ cup currants**
> **¹/₂ cup candied citron**
> **Grated rind of 1 lemon**
> **¹/₂ teaspoon ground cinnamon**
> **¹/₂ teaspoon ground cloves**
> **¹/₂ teaspoon ground cardamom**
> **6 cups white bread flour**

SECOND PROOF AND BAKING

1. Measure the culture into a large mixing bowl. Melt the butter over moderate heat, add the milk to the butter, and warm (to 75° to 85°). Add the salt and stir until dissolved. Add the raisins, currants, citron, lemon rind, cinnamon, cloves, and cardamom. Add this mixture to the culture and mix well.

2. Add the flour, 1 cup at a time, stirring until it is too stiff to mix by hand. Turn onto a floured board and knead in remaining flour until dough is satiny.

3. Form an oblong loaf.

4. Place on a baking sheet and proof, covered, at 85° for 1 to 2 hours, or until about doubled in bulk.

5. Preheat oven to 375°. Bake for 50 to 55 minutes.

6. Remove loaf from baking sheet and cool on a wire rack. You may top the loaf with a glaze of your choice while it is still warm.

Cinnamon Rolls

Makes 12 to 14 rolls

These rolls are lighter if all-purpose flour is used.

2 cups culture from the first proof (page 37)

$^1/_2$ cup milk

1 teaspoon pure vanilla extract

1 teaspoon salt

4 tablespoons sugar

3 cups white all-purpose flour

2 teaspoons cinnamon

2 tablespoons butter, melted

$^1/_2$ cup raisins

GLAZE I
2 tablespoons butter, melted

GLAZE II
1 cup confectioners' sugar

4 teaspoons hot milk

$^1/_2$ teaspoon pure vanilla extract

SECOND PROOF AND BAKING

1. Measure the culture into a large mixing bowl. Add milk, vanilla, salt, and 2 tablespoons of the sugar to the culture and mix well.

2. Add the flour, 1 cup at a time, stirring until it is too stiff to mix by hand. Turn onto a floured board and knead in remaining flour until dough is satiny.

3. Roll into a rectangle about $^1/_2$ inch thick. Combine the cinnamon with the remaining 2 tablespoons of sugar. Brush the surface of the dough with melted butter and sprinkle with the sugar-cinnamon mixture and the raisins.

4. Roll up the rectangle from the long side and slice into 1-inch-thick rolls. Place rolls on a baking sheet, close together, and proof, covered, at 85° for 1 to 2 hours.

5. Preheat oven to 400°. Bake for 25 to 30 minutes.

6. While rolls are hot, brush the tops with melted butter, or combine the confectioners' sugar, hot milk, and vanilla and drizzle over the rolls. If glaze is too stiff, add more milk, a few drops at a time.

Swedish Christmas Bread

Makes 2 loaves

One glance tells you this one's a heavyweight. Try making it with our new culture from Finland (page 175), but not when you're in a hurry.

> **4 cups culture from the first proof (page 37)**
> **2 tablespoons butter**
> **2 teaspoons salt**
> **¹/₂ cup molasses**
> **1 cup beer**
> **¹/₂ cup candied fruit peel**
> **2 tablespoons anise seed**
> **3 cups rye flour**
> **3 cups white bread flour**

SECOND PROOF AND BAKING

1. Measure the culture into a large mixing bowl. Melt the butter over moderate heat. Add the salt, molasses, and beer and stir until dissolved. Add the candied fruit peel and anise. Add this mixture to the culture and mix well.

2. Add the rye flour and mix well. Add the white flour, 1 cup at a time, stirring until it is too stiff to mix by hand. Turn onto a floured board and knead in remaining flour until dough is satiny.

3. Divide dough in half and form 2 balls.

4. Form oblong loaves.

5. Place in loaf pans and proof, covered, at 85° for 1¹/₂ to 3 hours. When dough rises 1 to 2 inches above the edges of the pan, it is ready to bake.

6. Preheat oven to 375°. Bake for 50 minutes.

7. Remove loaves from pans and cool on wire racks.

Salted Pretzels

Makes 15 to 20 pretzels

Sourdough makes these basic partners for beer and spicy mustard a special treat.

2 cups culture from the first proof (page 37)

2 tablespoons oil

1 teaspoon salt

1 tablespoon sugar

$1/2$ cup warm water (75° to 85°)

3 cups white bread flour

$1/4$ cup baking soda

Coarse salt

SECOND PROOF AND BAKING

1. Measure the culture into a large mixing bowl. Add the oil, salt, and sugar to the warm water and mix well. Add to the culture and mix.

2. Add the flour, 1 cup at a time, stirring until it is too stiff to mix by hand. Turn onto a floured board and knead in remaining flour until dough is satiny.

3. Form into egg-sized balls.

4. Roll each ball between the hands to form a 14-inch rope.

5. Twist and loop the ropes into pretzel shapes and proof, covered, at 85° for 1 hour.

6. Bring a large pan of water to a boil. Stir in the baking soda. Drop the pretzels carefully, one at a time, into the boiling water. Simmer briefly, turning once. Remove them with a slotted spoon and place on cloth or paper towels until the water drains off.

7. Preheat oven to 425°. Transfer pretzels to a baking sheet, make several oblique slashes in the crusts with a razor blade, and sprinkle with coarse salt.

8. Bake for 30 to 40 minutes, or until brown.

Breadsticks

Makes about 20 breadsticks, depending on size

You should pull and roll these sticks of dough until they reach the length you prefer. They can be as long and thin or as short and fat as you like. The thicker sticks are chewy; the thinner ones are crisp. They freeze well in plastic freezer bags, and heat in seconds in the microwave. A mixture of sticks, each coated with a different seed or with coarse salt, is delicious with cocktails or beer.

> **2 cups culture from the first proof (page 37)**
> **1 tablespoon butter**
> **¹/₂ cup milk**
> **1 teaspoon salt**
> **1 tablespoon sugar**
> **3 cups white bread flour**
>
> **GLAZE**
> **2 eggs, beaten**
> **Poppy or sesame seeds, or coarse salt**

SECOND PROOF AND BAKING

1. Measure the culture into a large mixing bowl. Melt the butter over moderate heat, add the milk to the butter, and warm (to 75° to 85°). (Or mix the butter and milk together and warm in a microwave oven.) Add the salt and sugar and stir until dissolved. Add this mixture to the culture and mix well.

2. Add the flour, 1 cup at a time, stirring until it is too stiff to mix by hand. Turn onto a floured board and knead in remaining flour until dough is satiny.

3. Divide dough into approximately 20 small balls.

4. Roll each ball into a rope about ¹/₄ to ¹/₂ inch in diameter.

5. Arrange 1 inch apart on a baking sheet and proof, covered, at 85° for 30 minutes, or until they start to rise.

6. Preheat oven to 375°. Brush breadsticks with egg and sprinkle with seed or salt.

7. Bake for 15 minutes, or until uniformly brown.

Caraway Crunches

Makes 16

These sourdough snacks will disappear in a hurry. Fortunately, you can just as easily double the recipe.

2 cups culture from the first proof (page 37)
1 tablespoon butter
¹/₂ cup milk
1 teaspoon salt
1 tablespoon sugar
3 cups white bread flour

GLAZE
2 eggs, beaten
2 tablespoons caraway seeds

SECOND PROOF AND BAKING

1. Measure the culture into a large mixing bowl. Melt the butter over moderate heat, add the milk to the butter, and warm (to 75° to 85°). (Or mix the butter and milk together and warm in a microwave oven.) Add the salt and sugar and stir until dissolved. Add this mixture to the culture and mix well.

2. Add the flour, 1 cup at a time, stirring until it is too stiff to mix by hand. Turn onto a floured board and knead in remaining flour until dough is satiny.

3. Divide dough in half and form 2 balls.

4. Roll each ball into a rectangle approximately 12 × 18 inches.

5. Cut the rectangles in half the long way.

6. Cut each half into squares or rectangles and then into triangles.

7. Brush the triangles with the egg and sprinkle with caraway seeds.

8. Roll up the triangles from the long side and place on a baking sheet.

9. Proof, covered, at 85° for 30 to 60 minutes.

10. Preheat oven to 375°. Bake for 20 minutes.

Pizza

Makes four 12- to 13-inch pizzas

Sourdough pizza is different. It's not the topping but the dough and crust that will blow your mind. Don't try it unless you're prepared for addiction. It's best to use a fast culture (such as the Russian culture available from Sourdoughs International [page 176]) to produce just the right amount of leavening in quick order.

2 cups culture from the first proof (page 37)

1 teaspoon salt

$^1/_2$ cup warm water (75° to 85°)

2 tablespoons oil

3 cups white bread flour

Cornmeal or semolina

Pizza toppings of your choice

SECOND PROOF AND BAKING

1. Measure the culture into a large mixing bowl. Dissolve the salt in the warm water, add the oil, and mix briefly. Add this to the culture and mix in well.

2. Add the flour, 1 cup at a time, stirring until it is too stiff to mix by hand. Turn onto a well-floured board and knead in the remaining flour until dough is satiny.

3. Divide the dough into 4 equal portions and form into balls.

4. With a rolling pin, flatten the balls into 12- to 13-inch rounds about $1/8$ inch thick.

5. Fold each round in half and transfer to a baker's peel or thin baking sheet sprinkled with cornmeal or semolina. Unfold and pinch a rim about $1/2$ inch high around the edge.

6. Proof, covered, for about 45 minutes at 85°.

7. Place a baking stone in a cold oven and preheat for at least 15 minutes at 450° to 500°.

8. Add the toppings to the rounds of dough and transfer the pizzas to the hot baking stone (see Note).

9. Bake for 20 to 25 minutes, or until crust is brown. Remove from the oven with the baker's peel.

NOTE: It takes practice to transfer the pizza to the stone. As an alternative, bake the pizza on a traditional pizza pan sprinkled with cornmeal, or, for a better crust, place the pizza pan on a hot baking stone. Cornmeal on the stone is not necessary for this method.

Bagels

Makes 15 bagels

You probably think you've eaten sourdough bagels sometime, but unless you made them yourself they probably weren't genuine sourdough. Try these and you won't forget them.

2 cups culture from the first proof (page 37)

2 eggs, beaten

2 tablespoons oil

$\frac{1}{2}$ cup milk

2 tablespoons sugar

1 teaspoon salt

3 cups white bread flour

2 tablespoons sugar

SECOND PROOF AND BAKING

1. Measure the culture into a large mixing bowl. Add eggs, oil, milk, sugar, and salt to the culture and mix well.

2. Add the flour, 1 cup at a time, stirring until it is too stiff to mix by hand. Turn onto a floured board and knead in remaining flour until dough is satiny. Use additional flour if needed.

3. Divide into 15 equal balls.

4. Roll each ball into a 6-inch rope and pinch the ends together, forming a dough-nut shape.

5. Proof, covered, at 85° for 1 hour.

6. Bring 4 quarts of water to a boil and add 2 tablespoons of sugar. Drop the bagels, 2 at a time, into the water. Remove them after they rise to the surface, drain on paper towels, and place on a baking sheet.

7. Preheat oven to 375°. Bake for 25 to 30 minutes.

8. Cool on wire racks.

Cheese Brioche

Makes 2 loaves

Brioches are uniquely French creations; they are extremely light. This is hardly the forte of sourdoughs, but try it. You will be surprised. Brioches are usually baked in special molds. I use the French culture (from Sourdoughs International, page 175) to produce a special cheese brioche as either a molded or braided loaf.

2 cups culture from the first proof (page 37)

2 tablespoons sugar

1 teaspoon salt

4 ounces Gruyère cheese, grated

4 cups white bread flour

6 eggs

1 cup butter

1 egg yolk beaten with 2 teaspoons water

SECOND PROOF AND BAKING

1. Measure the culture into a large mixing bowl. Add the sugar, salt, cheese, and 2 cups of the flour to the culture and mix well.

2. Mix in the eggs, 1 at a time.

3. Add the remaining 2 cups flour and mix well. Turn out on a well-floured board. The dough will be very soft and sticky. Knead the dough, using your hands and a dough scraper, until it loses its stickiness and becomes elastic, about 10 minutes.

4. Break off walnut-sized pieces of butter and, using a spatula or dough scraper, fold them one at a time into the dough. Knead until the dough is smooth.

5. To form traditional brioches, divide into 2 equal balls. Put in greased brioche molds (or try a Bundt cake pan). Make 2 or 3 diagonal slashes in tops of loaves. Or make 2 braided loaves following the instructions on page 61.

6. Proof, covered, at 85° for 3 to 4 hours, or until at least doubled in bulk.

7. Preheat oven to 400°. Brush with egg yolk glaze.

8. Bake for 30 minutes, or until brown. Remove loaves from pans and cool on wire racks.

Crumpets

Makes 8

Crumpets are as English as Big Ben. The batter is beaten vigorously to develop the gluten needed for leavening as the crumpet dough is proofed. Crumpets can be cooked free-form, like pancakes, but the traditional method is to pour the batter into 3- or 4-inch rings.

2 cups culture from the first proof (page 37)
1/4 cup butter
1/2 teaspoon salt
1 egg, beaten
1 cup white bread flour

SECOND PROOF AND BAKING

1. Measure the culture into a large mixing bowl. Melt the butter over moderate heat or in the microwave. Add the salt and egg and stir until mixed well. Add this mixture to the culture and mix well for several minutes.

2. Add the flour and mix well to fully develop the gluten.

3. Proof, covered, at 85° for 1 hour.

4. Preheat an oiled griddle and oiled crumpet rings to a moderate temperature. Crumpet rings can be made from a can 1 1/2 inches high from which the top and bottom have been cut.

5. Pour or spoon batter into rings, filling them one-third full.

6. Cook for 5 to 7 minutes, or until holes appear in the dough.

7. Remove rings and turn crumpets over and cook the other side for about 2 minutes.

8. Cool on wire racks.

Barm Brack

Makes 2 loaves

Barm means homemade yeast, and this recipe, which is popular in southern Ireland, is nearly perfect for sourdough.

> **4 cups culture from the first proof (page 37)**
>
> **1 cup butter**
>
> **1 cup milk**
>
> **2 teaspoons salt**
>
> **1 cup firmly packed brown sugar**
>
> **4 eggs, beaten**
>
> **$^1/_2$ teaspoon ground nutmeg**
>
> **1 tablespoon caraway seeds**
>
> **6 cups white bread flour**

SECOND PROOF AND BAKING

1. Measure the culture into a large mixing bowl. Melt the butter over moderate heat, add the milk to the butter, and warm (to 75° to 85°). Add the salt, brown sugar, eggs, nutmeg, and caraway seeds and stir. Add this mixture to the culture and mix well.

2. Add the flour, 1 cup at a time, stirring until it is too stiff to mix. Turn onto a floured board and knead in remaining flour until dough is satiny.

3. Divide the dough in half, form loaves, and place in two loaf pans.

4. Proof, covered, at 85°, for 1 to 2 hours, until dough rises to the tops of the pans.

5. Preheat oven to 350°. Bake for 50 to 55 minutes.

6. Cool loaves in the pans.

Caraway Croissant Rolls

Makes 12 rolls

Sourdough croissants? You bet! These ones with caraway are great and have a distinct sourdough taste.

2 cups culture from the first proof (page 37)

$^1/_2$ cup milk

$^1/_4$ cup oil

1 teaspoon salt

2 teaspoons sugar

1 egg, beaten

$3^1/_2$ cups white bread flour

GLAZE
1 egg, beaten
2 tablespoons milk
Caraway seeds

SECOND PROOF AND BAKING

1. Measure the culture into a large mixing bowl. Add milk, oil, salt, sugar, and egg to the culture and mix well.

2. Add the flour, 1 cup at a time, stirring until it is too stiff to mix by hand. Turn onto a floured board and knead in remaining flour until dough is satiny.

3. Divide dough into 2 balls and roll into flat rounds about 16 inches in diameter and $^1/_4$ inch thick.

4. Cut rounds in half and then cut each half into thirds to make triangles.

5. Roll up triangles from the periphery to the point and bend to form crescents.

6. Combine the beaten egg with the milk for the glaze.

7. Brush the rolls with milk-egg mixture and roll in caraway seeds.

8. Place on an oiled baking sheet and proof, covered, at 85° for 1 to 2 hours.

9. Preheat oven to 425°. Bake for 25 to 30 minutes.

Poppy Seed Rolls

Makes 12 rolls

This is a good recipe. Once in a while when I end up with extra dough from almost anything, I'll make these rolls.

    2 cups culture from the first proof (page 37)

    $1/2$ cup milk

    2 tablespoons oil

    1 teaspoon salt

    2 teaspoons sugar

    1 egg, beaten

    3 cups white bread flour

    GLAZE

    1 egg, beaten

    2 tablespoons milk

    Poppy seeds

SECOND PROOF AND BAKING

1. Measure the culture into a large mixing bowl. Add milk, oil, salt, sugar, and egg to culture and mix well.

2. Add the flour, 1 cup at a time, stirring until it is too stiff to mix by hand. Turn onto a floured board and knead in remaining flour until dough is satiny.

3. Divide the dough into 12 equal balls.

4. Form a flattened oval roll from each ball and place on a baking sheet. Combine beaten egg and milk, and brush this mixture on the rolls. Sprinkle with poppy seeds.

5. Make a cross slash in the top of each roll.

6. Proof, covered, at 85° for 1 to 2 hours.

7. Preheat oven to 425°. Bake for 20 to 25 minutes or until brown.

Whole Wheat Muffins

Makes 12-14

These hearty muffins will probably work best with a fast culture (such as our Russian culture, page 176).

2 cups culture from the first proof (page 37)

1 egg, beaten

$^1/_2$ cup milk

2 tablespoons sugar

1 teaspoon salt

$^1/_4$ cup butter

2 cups whole wheat flour

1 cup white bread flour

SECOND PROOF AND BAKING

1. Measure the culture into a large mixing bowl. Add the egg, milk, sugar, and salt to the culture and mix.

2. Mix the flours together thoroughly. With a fork, cut the butter into the flours until the mixture is finely granular.

3. Add to the culture mixture and stir until it is just moist, but not lump-free.

4. Spoon batter into muffin tins or drop spoonfuls on a sheet (see Note) and proof, covered, at 85° for 1 hour.

5. Preheat oven to 400°. Bake for 20 minutes, or until brown

NOTE: If muffin tins are not used, the batter must be thicker.

Butterflake Rolls

Makes 8 rolls

This is a fun, buttery breakfast treat with delicious sourdough flavor.

> 2 cups culture from the first proof (page 37)
>
> 1 egg, beaten
>
> 3/4 cup butter, melted
>
> 1 teaspoon salt
>
> 1 tablespoon sugar
>
> 1/2 cup milk
>
> 3 cups white bread flour
>
> **GLAZE**
>
> 1 egg, beaten
>
> Sesame seeds

SECOND PROOF AND BAKING

1. Measure the culture into a large mixing bowl. Add the beaten egg, 1/4 cup of the melted butter, salt, and sugar to the milk and mix briefly. Add to the culture and mix.

2. Add the flour, 1 cup at a time, stirring until it is too stiff to mix by hand. Turn onto a floured board and knead in remaining flour until dough is satiny.

3. Divide dough into 8 equal balls.

4. Dust each ball lightly with flour and flatten to a thin oval approximately 18 inches in the longest dimension.

5. Brush each oval with some of the remaining 1/2 cup melted butter and roll into a tight "rope" from the long side. Roll the ropes back and forth until they double in length.

6. Coil each rope into a round and flatten gently with your hand or rolling pin into an 8-inch round.

7. Place on baking sheet, cover lightly, and proof, covered, at 85° for 1 hour.

8. Preheat oven to 400°. Brush rolls with beaten egg, sprinkle with sesame seeds, and bake for 12 to 15 minutes, or until brown.

Spiced Buns

Makes 10 buns

Spiced buns are perfect for an afternoon tea or bridge game

2 cups culture from the first proof (page 37)
¹/₂ cup milk
1 egg, beaten
1 teaspoon salt
1 tablespoon oil
1 teaspoon anise seed, crushed
1 cup rye flour
3 cups white bread flour

GLAZE
2 tablespoons milk
2 teaspoons caraway or cumin seeds

SECOND PROOF AND BAKING

1. Measure the culture into a large mixing bowl. Add milk, egg, salt, oil, and anise seed to the culture and mix well.

2. Add rye flour and mix well.

3. Add the white flour, 1 cup at a time stirring until it is too stiff to mix by hand. Turn onto a floured board and knead in remaining flour until dough is satiny.

4. Divide dough into 10 equal balls and flatten to 1¹/₂-inch rounds.

5. Place on a baking sheet, and brush tops with milk and sprinkle with caraway or cumin seeds.

6. Proof, covered, at 85° for 1 to 2 hours.

7. Preheat oven to 425°. Bake for 20 to 30 minutes.

Sourdough Biscuits

Makes 15 biscuits

Sourdough makes marvelous biscuits. Mix and knead this dough very briefly, just to moisten the flour. It will be sticky and you will need to dust it with flour occasionally when handling it. When cutting the biscuits, make a quick, sharp cut to avoid tearing the gluten and produce better rising. Place the biscuits close together on the baking sheet so they will rise together and seal their adjacent cut edges.

Most conventional biscuit recipes specify "cutting" the shortening into the dry ingredients with a fork or pastry blender. Most sourdough recipes, like this one, do not.

> 2 cups culture from the first proof (page 37)
> 1 cup white bread flour or all-purpose flour
> 1 tablespoon sugar
> $^1/_2$ teaspoon salt
> 1 teaspoon baking soda
> 2 tablespoons butter, melted

SECOND PROOF AND BAKING

1. Measure the culture into a large mixing bowl. Mix the flour, sugar, salt, and baking soda together thoroughly. Add to the culture and stir very briefly.

2. Turn onto a floured board and knead briefly, until the dough is soft and barely sticky. Add additional flour if needed.

3. Using a floured rolling pin or your hands, roll or pat the dough to a thickness of about $^1/_2$ inch, and cut biscuits with a biscuit cutter.

4. Place on a baking sheet close together, and brush tops with melted butter.

5. Proof, covered, at 85° for 1 hour.

6. Preheat oven to 375°. Bake for 20 to 25 minutes.

7. Serve hot.

Hamburger Buns

Makes 8 buns

You won't find these at the fast-food chains. Burgers on these buns are truly sublime.

2 cups culture from the first proof (page 37)
3 tablespoons butter
$1/2$ cup warm milk
2 eggs, beaten
1 teaspoon salt
2 tablespoons sugar
3 cups white bread flour

SECOND PROOF AND BAKING

1. Measure the culture into a large mixing bowl. Melt the butter. Add the milk, eggs, salt, and sugar and beat with a fork to mix. Add to the culture.

2. Add the flour, 1 cup at a time, stirring until it is too stiff to mix by hand. Turn onto a floured board and knead in remaining flour until dough is satiny.

3. Roll to a thickness of $1/2$ inch and cut with a 4-inch round cutter.

4. Place on a baking sheet and proof, covered, at 85° for 2 to 4 hours, or until doubled in bulk.

5. Preheat oven to 350°. Bake 15 to 18 minutes.

6. Remove buns from baking sheet and cool on a wire rack.

Caraway Hot Dog Buns

Makes about 20 buns

You can make short, conventional buns or the long ones, up to 9 or 10 inches, by simply rolling and pulling this dough into the desired length. The sourdough caraway flavor is purely delicious!

> **4 cups culture from the first proof (page 37)**
> **2 tablespoons butter**
> **1 cup milk**
> **2 teaspoons salt**
> **1 tablespoon caraway seeds**
> **2 tablespoons sugar**
> **6 cups white bread flour**

SECOND PROOF AND BAKING

1. Measure the culture into a large mixing bowl. Melt the butter over moderate heat, add the milk to the butter, and warm (to 75° to 85°). Add the salt, caraway seeds, and sugar and stir. Add this mixture to the culture and mix well.

2. Add the flour, 1 cup at a time, stirring until it is too stiff to mix by hand. Turn onto a floured board and knead in remaining flour until dough is satiny.

3. Divide dough into 20 equal pieces.

4. Roll each piece into a rope about 6 inches long.

5. Proof on baking sheets, covered, at 85° for 1 to 2 hours, or until about doubled in bulk.

6. Preheat oven to 375°. Bake for 35 minutes.

7. Remove buns from baking sheets and cool on wire racks.

Kaahk Ramazan

Makes 24 kaahks

Kaahks are usually baked in a crescent shape, the symbol of the Ottoman (Turkish) Empire. They are most popular during the holy period of Ramadan and are eaten after the daily period of fasting. This is not a simple recipe, but the results are worth the effort.

2 cups culture from the first proof (page 37)

2 teaspoons salt

3 tablespoons sugar

$^1/_2$ cup milk

2 teaspoons ground cinnamon

1 teaspoon pure vanilla extract

2 eggs, beaten

4 cups white bread flour

6 tablespoons butter

GLAZE
1 egg, beaten
1 tablespoon sesame or poppy seeds

SECOND PROOF AND BAKING

1. Measure the culture into a large mixing bowl. Add the salt and sugar to the milk, warm (to 75° to 85°) and stir to dissolve.

2. Add the cinnamon and vanilla to the beaten eggs. Stir and add the milk mixture.

3. Add the milk-egg mixture to the culture and mix well.

4. Add the flour, 1 cup at a time, stirring until it is too stiff to mix by hand. Turn onto a floured board and knead in remaining flour until smooth and satiny.

5. Divide in half and form 2 balls. Chill for 1 hour in refrigerator.

6. Place 3 tablespoons of the butter between 2 sheets of waxed paper and flatten with a rolling pin to an oval about 6 by 8 inches. Prepare a second oval with

the remaining 3 tablespoons butter and place both in the refrigerator to chill for 1 hour.

7. On a floured board, roll each ball of chilled dough into a flattened oval about 12 × 16 inches.

8. Place one piece of chilled, flattened butter in the center of each dough oval and fold the dough over the butter from all sides.

9. Roll each dough oval into a rectangle about 12 × 16 inches. Fold the bottom half up to the center and the top half down to the center. Repeat this rolling and folding once. Chill for 15 minutes.

10. Roll into a rectangle about 12 × 16 inches.

11. Cut each rectangle in half the long way, then cut each half into 3 equal squares. Sourdough is difficult to roll into an exact shape, but the objective is to form approximate squares for the next step. The size will determine the size of the finished rolls.

12. Cut the squares diagonally to form triangles, and roll up the triangles tightly from the broad side to the tip. Pull into a crescent shape and lightly pinch the tips together.

13. Place on a baking sheet and proof, covered, at 85° for 1 to 2 hours, or until they have doubled in size.

14. Gently separate the joined tips, brush with beaten egg, and sprinkle with sesame or poppy seeds.

15. Preheat oven to 425°. Bake for 10 to 15 minutes. Remove kaahks from baking sheet and cool on wire racks.

Psomi

Makes 2 loaves

This is the Greek equivalent of a French bread. Placing a pan filled with boiling water in the oven produces steam, which gives the bread a thick, chewy crust. Or try using a mister as described for French bread (page 52).

> 2 cups culture from the first proof (page 37)
> 2 teaspoons salt
> 2 tablespoons sugar
> 1 tablespoon butter, melted
> $^1\!/_2$ cup warm water (75° to 85°)
> 4 cups white bread flour
> 1 tablespoon fine white cornmeal

SECOND PROOF AND BAKING

1. Measure the culture into a large mixing bowl. Add salt, sugar, melted butter, and water to the culture and mix well.

2. Add the flour to the culture, 1 cup at a time, stirring until it is too stiff to mix by hand. Turn onto a floured board and knead in remaining flour until dough is satiny.

3. Divide dough into 2 equal balls.

4. Form into elongate loaves and place on a baking sheet sprinkled with white cornmeal.

5. Proof, covered, at 85° for 1 to 2 hours, or until about doubled in bulk.

6. Preheat oven to 400°. Make several diagonal slashes in tops of loaves with a razor blade.

7. Immediately before baking, pour boiling water into a baking pan placed on lowest level of oven to create steam. Remove water after first 15 minutes.

8. Bake 40 to 45 minutes. Remove loaves from baking sheets and cool on wire racks.

Naun

Makes 8 to 10 rolls

Naun is leavened Afghanistan whole wheat bread. The wild yeast ferments this heavy dough to produce surprisingly light rolls of breakfast bread.

> **2 cups culture from the first proof (page 37)**
> **1½ teaspoons salt**
> **½ cup water**
> **1 cup white bread flour**
> **2 cups whole wheat flour**

SECOND PROOF AND BAKING

1. Measure the culture into a large mixing bowl. Add salt and water to the culture and mix well.

2. Combine the flours, mix well, and add to the culture, 1 cup at a time, stirring until it is too stiff to mix by hand. Turn onto a floured board and knead in remaining flour mixture until dough is satiny.

3. Oil hands and divide dough into 8 to 10 equal balls.

4. Flatten with hands or an oiled rolling pin and form elongate ovals ½ inch thick. Place on baking sheet.

5. Proof, covered, at 85° for 1 to 2 hours or until doubled in bulk.

6. With an oiled finger, make three parallel grooves about ½ inch deep on the surface of each roll.

7. Preheat oven to 450°. Bake for 15 to 20 minutes. Remove rolls from baking sheet and cool on wire racks.

Khobz with Hilbeh

Makes 10 flatbreads

Khobz is a whole wheat flatbread. The whole wheat dough is slightly leavened during the final proof to produce a puffed bread. Hilbeh is a fenugreek-based spread widely used by the Arabs on flatbreads. Fenugreek is a somewhat bitter seed with an odor resembling celery. Look for it in ethnic food shops. The Hilbeh will keep for several weeks in the refrigerator.

> **2 cups culture from the first proof (page 37)**
>
> **1 teaspoon salt**
>
> **$^1/_2$ cup water**
>
> **3 cups whole wheat flour**
>
> **1 recipe Hilbeh (recipe follows)**

SECOND PROOF AND BAKING

1. Measure the culture into a large mixing bowl. Add the salt and water to the culture. Mix briefly and add the flour, 1 cup at a time, stirring until it is too stiff to mix by hand. Turn out onto a floured board and gradually add the remaining flour, kneading until dough is smooth.

2. Form 10 balls about $1^1/_2$ inches in diameter. Proof, covered, at 85° for 4 hours, or until doubled in bulk.

3. Roll balls out to 4-inch rounds, cover with a cloth or plastic, and let rise for 30 minutes on a lightly floured board.

4. Oil and heat a heavy pan or griddle until just short of smoking hot.

5. Cook the rounds for 1 minute on each side.

6. Serve warm with Hilbeh.

NOTE: Khobz can also be served with honey.

Hilbeh

2 teaspoons fenugreek seeds

Cold water

2 cloves garlic

¹/₄ cup chopped cilantro

¹/₂ teaspoon salt

2 teaspoons lemon juice

1 small, hot chile, seeds removed (optional)

1. Soak fenugreek seeds in ¹/₂ cup cold water for 12 to 18 hours, until there is a jelly-like coating on the seeds. Drain.

2. Place all ingredients in a blender with enough cold water to make a paste. Blend.

3. Store covered in refrigerator.

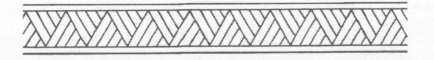

Saluf

Makes 10 flatbreads

This is a lightly leavened flatbread typical of Arab breads. Its flavor comes from the 12-hour proof. Unlike many Arab breads, this one does not puff to form a pocket.

2 cups culture from the first proof (page 37)
$1/2$ cup water
$1/2$ teaspoon salt
$1^1/2$ cups whole wheat flour
$1^1/2$ cups white bread flour

SECOND PROOF AND BAKING

1. Measure the culture into a large mixing bowl. Add the water and salt to the culture and mix well.

2. Combine the flours, mix well, and add to the culture, 1 cup at a time, stirring until it is too stiff to mix by hand. Turn onto a floured board and knead in remaining flour mixture until dough is satiny.

3. Divide dough into 10 equal balls.

4. Flatten by hand or with rolling pin and form ovals $1/2$ inch thick and 6 inches in diameter. Prick surface with a fork (or make holes with fingers, as they do in Arabia).

5. Lightly brush baking sheet with oil. Preheat oven and baking sheet to 550°.

6. Brush tops of flatbreads lightly with oil. Use a lightly floured baker's peel or metal spatula to transfer 2 rounds to the heated baking sheet.

7. Bake for 4 to 5 minutes until tops are lightly browned. If the rounds puff up to form a pocket, press lightly with a fork. Repeat with remaining rounds.

8. Serve warm. To enjoy these as the Arabs do, spread them with Hilbeh (page 111).

Mafrooda

Makes 10 flatbreads

This white flatbread is not allowed to form a pouch. Press with the tines of a fork during baking if it starts to puff.

> **2 cups culture from the first proof (page 37)**
> **1¹/₂ teaspoons salt**
> **1 teaspoon sugar**
> **2 tablespoons oil**
> **¹/₂ cup warm water (75° to 85°)**
> **4 cups white bread flour**

SECOND PROOF AND BAKING

1. Measure the culture into a large mixing bowl. Add salt, sugar, oil, and water to the culture and mix well.

2. Add the flour to the culture 1 cup at a time, stirring until it is too stiff to mix by hand. Turn onto a floured board and knead in remaining flour until dough is satiny.

3. Divide into 10 equal portions and form balls.

4. Preheat oven to 500°. Oil a baking sheet or griddle and preheat it in the oven. Flatten dough by hand or with a rolling pin into 10-inch rounds.

5. Use a floured baker's peel to transfer one round at a time to the preheated baking sheet or griddle.

6. Bake 4 to 5 minutes. Turn briefly to brown. Press with the tines of a fork if the breads puff up during baking.

NOTE: Rounds can also be cooked in an electric frying pan on the highest setting, with lid on. Heat pan until smoking hot.

Khubz Arabi (Arab bread)

Makes 8 pita breads

Khubz Arabi is a hollow flatbread. This is probably the most exciting and delicious pita I have ever encountered. It is produced throughout the Middle East, both commercially and in the home. It forms a soft, flat, white round bread with a pouch inside.

> **4 cups culture from the first proof (page 37)**
> **1 cup water**
> **1 teaspoon salt**
> **1 tablespoon sugar**
> **1 tablespoon oil**
> **5 cups white bread flour**
> **Cornmeal or semolina**

SECOND PROOF AND BAKING

1. Measure the culture into a large mixing bowl. Add water, salt, sugar, and oil to the culture and mix well

2. Add the flour, 1 cup at a time, stirring until it is too stiff to mix by hand. Turn onto a floured board and knead in remaining flour until dough is satiny.

3. Divide into 8 equal balls.

4. Roll the balls into flat rounds about $1/4$ inch thick and form two stacks, with the rounds separated by waxed paper or paper towels.

5. Proof the rounds, covered, at 85° for about 30 minutes.

6. Preheat oven and a baking stone or baking sheet to 500°.

7. Sprinkle the hot stone with cornmeal or semolina just before transferring pitas. Use a baker's peel or large spatula to slide rounds onto the heated stone. Use care to avoid damaging the surface or the rounds may not puff completely. Bake for about 5 minutes, or until rounds puff and start to brown.

8. Remove from oven with a spatula and cool on wire racks.

Khubz Saj (thin bread)

Makes 25 to 30 flatbreads

Khubz Saj is the bread of the village Arab and bedouin. It is still prepared in the camp-sites, over a fire of camel dung in a domed iron oven, called the saj. In the ancient method, the thin rounds are draped over a special pillow with a hand grip on the back. When the oven is very hot, the flat rounds are slapped onto the iron surface and removed within a minute or two. You can use a hot baking stone or metal baking sheet, as in the recipe for Khubz Arabi (page 114).

> **4 cups culture from the first proof (page 37)**
> **2 teaspoons salt**
> **1 tablespoon sugar**
> **1 cup warm water (75° to 85°)**
> **6 cups white bread flour**

Second Proof and Baking

1. Measure the culture into a large mixing bowl. Add salt, sugar, and water to the culture and mix well.

2. Add the flour, 1 cup at a time, stirring until it is too stiff to mix by hand. Turn onto a floured board and knead in remaining flour until dough is satiny.

3. Form into balls about 2 inches in diameter.

4. Preheat oven and a baking sheet or stone to 450°.

5. Roll the balls out quite thin. They should be about 10 inches in diameter. As each one is formed, transfer it with a baker's peel or spatula to the preheated baking sheet and bake for 3 minutes.

6. Remove from oven with a spatula and cool on wire racks.

Seasoned Flatbread

Makes 6 flatbreads

This flatbread can be varied endlessly with your favorite spices.

2 cups culture from the first proof (page 37)
1¹/₂ teaspoons salt
1 tablespoon sugar
2 tablespoons oil
2¹/₂ cups white bread flour

GLAZE
Olive oil
1 teaspoon each dried thyme and marjoram
1 teaspoon dried sumac (see Note)

SECOND PROOF AND BAKING

1. Measure the culture into a large mixing bowl. Add salt, sugar, and oil to the culture and mix well.

2. Add the flour to the culture, stirring until it is too stiff to mix by hand. Turn onto a floured board and knead in remaining flour until dough is satiny.

3. Divide into 6 equal portions and form into balls.

4. Flatten by hand or with a rolling pin into 10-inch rounds and place on a lightly floured cloth or paper towel. Cover with another cloth and let rise for 30 minutes.

5. Brush with olive oil and sprinkle with thyme, marjoram, and sumac.

6. Preheat oven and an oiled baking sheet or griddle to 500°.

7. Use floured baker's peel to transfer one round at a time to the preheated griddle or baking sheet.

8. Bake 4 to 5 minutes, until round puffs. Do not turn.

NOTE: Ground sumac is available in Middle Eastern markets. These breads can be cooked in an electric frying pan on the highest setting, with the lid on. Preheat frying pan until smoking hot.

Mannaeesh

Makes 10 puffs

Mannaeesh is a timeless Middle Eastern favorite. It is lightly leavened to produce a soft bread that puffs and forms a hollowed pouch into which all sorts of delicious things may be stuffed. This bread is fun to bake and fun to eat. If hamburgers had originated in Arabia, this would have been the bun.

4 cups culture from the first proof (page 37)

1 teaspoon salt

1 tablespoon sugar

1 cup warm water (75° to 85°)

5 cups white bread flour

5 tablespoons olive oil

1 teaspoon each dried thyme and marjoram

3 tablespoons sesame seeds

SECOND PROOF AND BAKING

1. Measure the culture into a large mixing bowl. Add salt and sugar to the warm water and stir briefly to dissolve. Add this mixture to the culture and mix well.

2. Add flour, 1 cup at a time, stirring until it is too stiff to mix by hand. Turn onto a floured board and knead in remaining flour until dough is satiny.

3. Divide into 10 equal balls.

4. Roll the balls into flat rounds about 1/4 inch thick.

5. Proof the rounds, covered, at 85° for 1 to 2 hours.

6. Mix the olive oil, thyme, marjoram, and sesame seeds together and spread some on the surface of each round.

7. Preheat the oven and baking sheet to 450° and using a baker's peel or large spatula, slide the rounds onto the heated baking sheet one or two at a time.

8. Bake for 5 to 10 minutes, until the rounds puff suddenly, forming a central cavity. Cool on wire racks.

Kamut Bread

Makes 2 loaves

Kamut may or may not have originated in ancient Egypt. Agronomists are inclined to classify it as a subtype of durum. Whatever it is called or related to, it imparts a distinctly nutty flavor to a sourdough loaf. Its relationship to durum is perhaps an explanation for its relatively poor gluten content. It can be substituted in any recipe for 1 cup of rye or whole wheat flour. If you use more than 1 cup, it is a good idea to add a little gluten flour (see page 31).

4 cups culture from the first proof (page 37)

1 cup water

2 teaspoons salt

2 tablespoons sugar

¼ cup oil

2 tablespoons caraway seeds

1 cup rye flour

1 cup Kamut flour

4 cups white bread flour

SECOND PROOF

1. Measure the culture into a large mixing bowl. Warm the water (to 75° to 85°) and add the salt, sugar, oil, and caraway seeds. Mix briefly and add to the culture.

2. Add the rye and Kamut flours and mix well.

3. Add the white flour, 1 cup at a time, until it is too stiff to mix by hand. Turn onto a floured board and knead in the remaining flour until dough is smooth and satiny.

4. Divide dough into 2 equal pieces. Form into loaves and place in loaf pans. Proof, covered, at 85° for 2 to 3 hours, or until dough rises 1 to 2 inches above the edges of the pans.

5. Preheat oven to 350°. Bake for 50 to 55 minutes.

6. Remove loaves from pans and cool on wire racks.

SPELT RECIPES

The six recipes that follow all use various combinations of white and whole spelt flours. Some also include rye and whole wheat flours. Note that spelt flours are said to have a short mixing tolerance, but I have not experienced this problem when I have used them. If your breads do not rise well, however, you may need to experiment with shorter mixing times.

   If you are allergic to wheat glutens, or are baking for someone who is, you may wish to use an all-spelt culture. However, you should be aware that medical research has not produced conclusive findings regarding the allergenic properties of spelt. Refer to page 23 for instructions for transferring your culture from a bread-flour base to a spelt-flour base.

Spelt Bread

Makes 2 loaves

Spelt is the other ancient grain and, like Kamut, makes an excellent addition to many sourdough breads. Try this recipe, or use spelt as a substitute or addition in rye and whole wheat breads. This is a good recipe to compare the qualities of spelt and Kamut.

4 cups culture from the first proof (page 37)

1 cup water

2 teaspoons salt

2 tablespoons sugar

¹/₄ cup oil

2 tablespoons caraway seeds

1 cup rye flour

1 cup spelt flour

4 cups white bread flour

SECOND PROOF

1. Measure the culture into a large mixing bowl. Warm the water (to 75° to 85°) and add the salt, sugar, oil, and caraway seeds. Mix briefly and add to the culture.

2. Add the rye and spelt flours and mix well.

3. Add the white flour, 1 cup at a time, stirring until it is too stiff to mix by hand. Turn onto a floured board and knead in the remaining flour until dough is smooth and satiny.

4. Divide dough into 2 equal pieces. Form into loaves and place in loaf pans. Proof, covered, at 85° for 2 to 3 hours, or until dough rises 1 to 2 inches above the edges of the pans.

5. Preheat oven to 350°. Bake 50 to 55 minutes.

6. Remove loaves from pans and cool on wire racks.

German Spelt Bread

Makes 2 loaves

In Europe, spelt is known as "dinkel." This recipe combines white and whole spelt with rye to produce a richness characteristic of German breads. You should try using both porter and stout beers, then compare the results.

> **4 cups culture from the first proof (page 37)**
> **2 tablespoons butter**
> **2 teaspoons salt**
> **2 tablespoons firmly packed brown sugar**
> **³/₄ cup malt beer**
> **2 cups rye flour**
> **2 cups whole spelt flour**
> **2 cups white spelt flour**

SECOND PROOF AND BAKING

1. Measure the culture into a large mixing bowl. Melt the butter in the microwave (or over moderate heat). Add the salt, brown sugar, and beer and stir until dissolved. Add this mixture to the culture and stir well.

2. Mix the rye flour with the whole spelt flour and stir into the culture, 1 cup at a time.

3. Add the white spelt flour, stirring until it is too stiff to mix by hand. Turn onto a board floured with the remaining white spelt flour, and knead in the remaining flour until dough is satiny.

4. Divide the dough in half and form 2 balls, then form into loaves.

5. Place in loaf pans and proof, covered, at 85° for 1¹/₂ to 3 hours.

6. Preheat oven to 375°. Bake for 50 to 55 minutes.

7. Remove loaves from pans and cool on wire racks.

Austrian Spelt Bread

Makes 2 loaves

We make the spelt breads in this book with organically grown spelt produced by Purity Foods under the label Vita-Spelt. This one with molasses and brown sugar has an exceptional flavor.

4 cups culture from the first proof (page 37)

2 teaspoons salt

2 tablespoons firmly packed brown sugar

³/₄ cup water

2 tablespoons molasses

2 tablespoons oil

1 tablespoon caraway seeds

2 tablespoons fennel seeds

1 cup medium rye flour

1 cup whole wheat flour

4 cups white spelt flour

SECOND PROOF AND BAKING

1. Measure the culture into a large mixing bowl. Dissolve the salt and brown sugar in the water. Add the molasses, oil, caraway seeds, and fennel seeds and mix well. Add this mixture to the culture and mix well.

2. Mix the rye and whole wheat flours together and add to the culture, 1 cup at a time.

3. Add the white spelt flour, 1 cup at a time, stirring until it is too thick to mix by hand. Turn onto a board covered with spelt flour and knead in the remaining white spelt flour until dough is satiny.

4. Divide into 2 halves and either place in loaf pans or form French loaves.

5. Proof, covered, at 85° for 2 to 3 hours, until about doubled in bulk.

6. Preheat oven to 375°. Bake for 50 to 55 minutes.

7. Remove loaves from pans and cool on wire racks.

A wild sourdough after culture preparation and ready for the first proof.

The Russian culture as it comes out of the refrigerator with a layer of "hooch" on the surface (left), two hours later when fully activated after proofing (center), and three more hours later when semidormant with bubble tracks on the jar indicating where the foam layer retreated (right).

When the dough looks like this, it is time to turn it out on a floured board and begin kneading.

The dough being kneaded
in this machine is
too stiff for effective
paddle action.

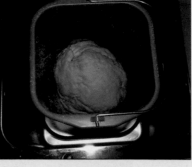

The dough is too thin to
rise well in the machine.

The proper consistency for
effective kneading in the
bread machine.

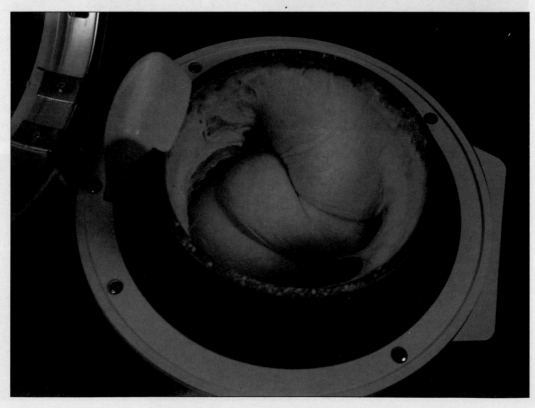

Caraway Spelt Bread

Makes 2 loaves

Spelt produces a reach creamy texture when added to a sourdough culture—the physical difference between this flour and wheat flours is immediately obvious. And the flavor of caraway with spelt is equally unique.

4 cups culture from the first proof (page 37)

³/₄ cup water

2 tablespoons butter, melted

1 teaspoon salt

2 tablespoons dark molasses

2 tablespoons caraway seeds

2 cups rye flour

4 cups white spelt flour

SECOND PROOF AND BAKING

1. Measure the culture into a large mixing bowl. Add water, butter, salt, molasses, and caraway seeds to the culture and mix.

2. Add the rye flour and mix. Add the spelt flour, 1 cup at a time, stirring until it is too stiff to mix by hand. Turn onto a board covered with spelt flour and knead in remaining spelt flour until dough is satiny.

3. Divide dough into 2 equal balls.

4. Press into flat oval rounds 1 inch thick and roll into loaves. Pinch seams as roll progresses.

5. Place in loaf pans and proof, covered, at 85° for 2 to 3 hours, or until doubled in bulk.

6. Preheat oven to 400°. Bake for 55 minutes. Remove loaves from pans and cool on wire racks.

Herb Spelt Bread

Makes 2 loaves

This recipe, which uses only white spelt flour, enables you to compare the leavening characteristics of spelt with those of wheat flours.

4 cups culture from the first proof (page 37)

³/₄ cup milk

2 tablespoons melted butter or oil

1 teaspoon salt

1 tablespoon sugar

1 teaspoon each dried thyme, oregano, and basil

6 cups white spelt flour

SECOND PROOF AND BAKING

1. Measure the culture into a large mixing bowl. Add the milk to the melted butter and warm (to 75° to 85°). Add the salt, sugar, and herbs and stir. Add this mixture to the culture and mix well.

2. Add the flour, 1 cup at a time, stirring until it is too stiff to mix by hand. Turn onto a board covered with spelt flour, and knead in remaining flour until dough is satiny.

3. Divide dough in half and form 2 balls.

4. Pat each ball into a 1-inch-thick oval and form loaves by rolling from the long side, pinching the seam together as you roll the dough to form the loaf.

5. Place the loaves on baking sheets and proof, covered, at 85° for 2 to 3 hours, or until about doubled in bulk.

6. Preheat oven to 375°. Bake for 55 to 60 minutes.

7. Remove loaves from baking sheets and cool on wire racks.

Spelt Cinnamon Rolls

Makes 12 to 14 rolls

Everyone knows what a standard cinnamon roll tastes like, but you haven't tasted really great ones until you've made them with spelt.

2 cups culture from the first proof (page 37)

$^1/_2$ cup milk

1 teaspoon pure vanilla extract

1 teaspoon salt

4 tablespoons sugar

3 cups white spelt flour

2 tablespoons butter, melted

2 teaspoons cinnamon

$^1/_2$ cup raisins

GLAZE 1
2 tablespoons butter, melted

GLAZE 2
1 cup confectioners' sugar

4 teaspoons hot milk

$^1/_2$ teaspoon pure vanilla extract

SECOND PROOF AND BAKING

1. Measure the culture into a large mixing bowl. Add milk, vanilla, salt, and 2 tablespoons of the sugar to the culture and mix well.

2. Add the flour, 1 cup at a time, stirring until it is too stiff to mix by hand. Turn onto a board covered with spelt flour and knead in remaining spelt flour until dough is satiny.

3. Roll into a rectangle about 1/2 inch thick. Brush the surface with melted butter. Combine the cinnamon with the remaining 2 tablespoons sugar, and sprinkle over the dough, along with the raisins.

4. Roll up the rectangle from the long side and cut into 1-inch-thick rolls. Place rolls on a baking sheet close together and proof, covered, at 85° for 1 to 2 hours.

5. Preheat oven to 400°. Bake for 25 to 30 minutes.

6. While rolls are hot, brush the tops with melted butter, or combine the ingredients for Glaze II and drizzle over the rolls. If the glaze is too stiff, add more milk, a few drops at a time.

DURUM RECIPES

You can use durum as a complete substitute for whole wheat flours in any recipe in this book, just be sure to review the information about the qualities of durum on pages 28–30. As with any whole wheat, better leavening will occur with about 50 percent white bread flour, but I have used durum with only 25 percent white flour successfully. The flavor of durum is hard to resist.

Durum World Bread

Makes 2 loaves

Use this recipe to sample the unique taste of durum without the masking flavors of other ingredients.

> **4 cups culture from the first proof (page 37)**
>
> **1 cup milk**
>
> **2 tablespoons melted butter or oil**
>
> **1 teaspoon salt**
>
> **2 tablespoons sugar**
>
> **3 cups durum flour**
>
> **3 cups white bread flour**
>
> **1 tablespoon melted butter**

SECOND PROOF AND BAKING

1. Measure the culture into a large mixing bowl. Add the milk to the 2 tablespoons of butter, warm briefly (to 75° to 85°), add the salt and sugar, and stir until dissolved. Add this mixture to the culture and mix well.

2. Add all the durum flour and mix. Add the bread flour, 1 cup at a time, stirring until the dough is too stiff to mix by hand. Turn onto a floured board and knead in the remaining bread flour until the dough is smooth and satiny. Divide the dough in half and form 2 balls.

3. Pat each ball into a 1-inch-thick oval and form loaves by rolling from the long side, pinching the seam together as you roll the dough to form the loaf.

4. Place in loaf pans and proof, covered, at 85° for 1½ to 3 hours. When the dough rises 1 to 2 inches above the edges of the pan, it is ready to bake.

5. Preheat oven to 375°. Bake for 10 minutes, reduce heat to 350°, and bake an additional 45 minutes.

6. After removing the bread from the oven, brush the crusts lightly with the remaining tablespoon of melted butter. Turn loaves out of pans and cool on a wire rack.

Durum Rye Bread

Makes 2 loaves

*I've raved about the taste of durum in bread, but you'll think I've understated its good-
ness when you try this recipe.*

4 cups culture from the first proof (page 37)

1 cup milk

2 teaspoons salt

¼ cup firmly packed brown sugar

2 tablespoons melted butter or oil

1 cup rye flour

2 cups durum flour

3 cups white bread flour

SECOND PROOF AND BAKING

1. Measure the culture into a large mixing bowl. Add milk, salt, sugar, and melted butter to the culture and mix well.

2. Add the rye and durum flours and mix. Add the white flour, 1 cup at a time, stirring until it is too stiff to mix by hand. Turn onto a floured board and knead in remaining flour until dough is satiny.

3. Form into 2 equal balls.

4. Pat or roll balls into flat rounds about 1½ inches thick. Form round loaves by folding in the middle; seal edges by pinching. Place on a baking sheet.

5. Proof, covered, at 85° for 3 to 4 hours, or until doubled in bulk.

6. Preheat oven to 375°. Make crisscross slashes in tops of loaves.

7. Bake for 55 to 60 minutes. Remove loaves from baking sheet and cool on a wire rack.

Durum Sunflower Bread

Makes 2 loaves

This is a somewhat heavier durum recipe. You may want to use the Russian sourdough to hurry it along.

> **4 cups culture from the first proof (page 37)**
>
> **1 cup milk**
>
> **2 tablespoons melted butter or oil**
>
> **2 teaspoons salt**
>
> **$^1/_2$ cup honey**
>
> **1 cup raw sunflower seeds**
>
> **2 cups durum flour**
>
> **2 cups whole wheat flour**
>
> **2 cups white bread flour**

SECOND PROOF AND BAKING

1. Measure the culture into a large mixing bowl. Add the milk to the butter and warm (to 75° to 85°). Add the salt, honey, and sunflower seeds. Add this mixture to the culture and mix well.

2. Add the durum and whole wheat flours and mix. Add the white flour, 1 cup at a time, stirring until it is too stiff to mix by hand. Turn onto a floured board and knead in remaining flour until dough is satiny.

3. Divide dough in half and form 2 balls.

4. Pat each ball into a 1-inch-thick oval and form loaves by rolling from the long side, pinching the seam together as you roll the dough to form the loaf.

5. Place in loaf pans and proof, covered, at 85° for 1$^1/_2$ to 3 hours. When dough rises 1 to 2 inches above the edges of the pans, it is ready to bake.

6. Preheat oven to 375°. Bake for 50 to 55 minutes.

7. Remove loaves from pans and cool on wire racks.

SOURDOUGH PANCAKES

Sourdough pancakes are fun and easy. The first 12-hour proof provides the flavor, but the pancakes will not rise well unless the wild yeast is fed again and given time to respond. Prospectors apparently never had that much time, and the genuine sourdough pancake is a thin, somewhat rubbery object that requires both an appetite and affection. There are generations of prospectors' descendants who consume rubbery pancakes and extol their virtues. You must try them for the experience, then form your own opinion.

If you allow an additional hour in the morning for the batter to have a quick leavening, your pancakes will be extraordinary. Without that hour, you can achieve the same effect by adding baking soda dissolved in warm water to the batter just before cooking the pancakes. Once the baking soda has been added, the batter must be used immediately. Don't use more than the specified amount of baking soda or the flavor will be neutralized. This is the ideal recipe in which to use a very fast culture (such as the Russian culture available from Sourdoughs International [page 176]) to leaven those cakes naturally.

Yukon Flapjacks

Makes 12 to 15 pancakes

Have the griddle piping hot before pouring on this batter. When a host of bubbles appears, it is time to turn the cakes over.

> **2 cups culture from the first proof (page 37)**
> **1 egg, beaten**
> **2 tablespoons oil**
> **2 tablespoons sugar**
> **$1/2$ teaspoon salt**
> **White bread flour as needed**
> **$1/2$ teaspoon baking soda**

SECOND PROOF AND BAKING

1. Measure the culture into a large mixing bowl. Add egg, oil, sugar, and salt to the culture and mix briefly.

2. Add enough flour to attain the desired consistency. Mix until lump-free.

3. Just before cooking the pancakes, dissolve baking soda in 1 tablespoon of warm water and gently blend into batter (see Note).

4. With a pitcher or ladle, pour 2- to 3-inch rounds on a hot (400°) griddle.

5. Cook 2 to 4 minutes, until bubbles form on surface. Turn and cook for an additional 2 minutes. Serve hot.

NOTE: If time permits, omit baking soda. Stir 1 cup white flour and $1/2$ cup of milk into batter. Proof, covered, for 1 hour at 85°.

Austrian Rye Pancakes

Makes about 12 pancakes

There isn't a combination of rye and sourdough that isn't good. When you're searching for something special for Sunday morning breakfast, these pancakes are what you want!

2 cups culture from the first proof (page 37)

1 egg, beaten

2 tablespoons butter, melted

¹/₂ cup milk

2 tablespoons sugar

1 teaspoon salt

1 cup rye flour

White bread flour as needed

¹/₂ teaspoon baking soda

SECOND PROOF AND BAKING

1. Measure the culture into a large mixing bowl. Add egg, melted butter, milk, sugar, and salt to the culture and mix briefly.

2. Add rye flour and then enough white flour to attain the desired pancake consistency. Mix until lump-free.

3. Just before cooking, dissolve baking soda in 1 tablespoon warm water and gently blend into the batter.

4. With a pitcher or ladle, pour 2- to 3-inch rounds on a hot (400°) griddle.

5. Cook 2 to 4 minutes, until bubbles form on surface. Turn and cook an additional 2 minutes. Serve hot.

NOTE: If time permits, omit baking soda. Stir 1 cup white flour and ¹/₂ cup of milk into batter. Proof, covered, for 1 hour at 85°.

Apple Pancakes

Makes 12 to 15 pancakes

Applesauce provides the flavor in this recipe. For a real treat, drop 2 fresh, peeled and cored apples in your food processor, chop to almost a purée, and substitute the purée for the applesauce.

2 cups culture from the first proof (page 37)

1 egg, beaten

$1/2$ cup smooth applesauce

2 tablespoons melted butter

1 tablespoon sugar

1 teaspoon salt

White bread flour as needed

$1/2$ teaspoon baking soda

SECOND PROOF AND BAKING

1. Measure the culture into a large mixing bowl. Add egg, applesauce, melted butter, sugar, and salt to the culture and mix briefly.

2. Add flour to attain desired consistency. Mix until lump-free.

3. Just before cooking, dissolve baking soda in 1 tablespoon warm water and gently blend into the batter.

4. With a pitcher or ladle, pour 2- to 3-inch rounds on a hot (400°) griddle.

5. Cook 2 to 4 minutes, until bubbles form on surface. Turn and cook for an additional 2 minutes. Serve hot.

NOTE: If time permits, omit baking soda. Stir 1 cup white flour and $1/2$ cup of milk into batter. Proof, covered, for 1 hour at 85°.

Maple Pancakes

Makes 12 to 15 pancakes

There are artificial maple flavorings, but none are an adequate substitute. Use the real stuff, especially in pancakes.

2 cups culture from the first proof (page 37)
1 egg, beaten
2 tablespoons butter, melted
¼ cup maple syrup
½ teaspoon salt
White bread flour as needed
½ teaspoon baking soda

SECOND PROOF AND BAKING

1. Measure the culture into a large mixing bowl. Add egg, melted butter, maple syrup, and salt to the culture and mix briefly.

2. Add flour to attain the desired consistency. Mix until lump-free.

3. Just before cooking, dissolve baking soda in 1 tablespoon warm water and gently blend into the batter.

4. With a pitcher or ladle, pour 2- to 3-inch rounds on a hot (400°) griddle.

5. Cook 2 to 4 minutes, until bubbles form on surface. Turn and cook for an additional 2 minutes. Serve hot.

NOTE: If time permits, omit baking soda. Stir 1 cup white flour and ½ cup of milk into batter. Proof, covered, for 1 hour at 85°.

SOURDOUGH WAFFLES

Sourdough waffles combine the unequaled flavor of the culture with the light texture of all good waffles. To achieve the latter, the eggs are separated and the whites are beaten to the soft peak stage. At the very last minute, just before baking, the whites are gently folded into the batter. Oil and preheat the waffle iron before pouring on the batter.

Yukon Sourdough Waffles

Makes 3 or 4 waffles

These waffles will be lighter and better if you can proof the batter for an hour at 85° just before adding the beaten egg whites. Use a fast culture (such as the Russian culture from Sourdoughs International [page 176]) for best results.

2 cups culture from the first proof (page 37)

2 eggs, separated

¼ cup milk

2 tablespoons butter, melted

1 tablespoon sugar

1 teaspoon salt

White bread flour as needed (about ½ to 1 cup)

SECOND PROOF AND BAKING

1. Measure the culture into a large mixing bowl. Add egg yolks, milk, melted butter, sugar, and salt to the culture and mix briefly.

2. Add flour to attain the desired consistency. Mix until lump-free. Proof, covered, for 1 hour at 85°.

3. Beat egg whites until they form soft peaks. Gently mix into the batter.

4. Preheat waffle iron. Pour some of the batter onto waffle iron and cook for 7 to 8 minutes. Repeat with remaining batter. Serve hot.

Rye Waffles

Makes 3 waffles

It's hard to say whether rye waffles are better than rye pancakes unless you've tried both. Twice!

> **2 cups culture from the first proof (page 37)**
>
> **2 eggs, separated**
>
> **$^1/_2$ cup milk**
>
> **2 tablespoons oil**
>
> **2 teaspoons sugar**
>
> **1 teaspoon salt**
>
> **$^1/_2$ cup rye flour**
>
> **White bread flour as needed (about $^1/_2$ to 1 cup)**
>
> **$^1/_2$ teaspoon baking soda**

SECOND PROOF AND BAKING

1. Measure the culture into a large mixing bowl. Add egg yolks, milk, oil, sugar, and salt to the culture and mix briefly.

2. Add rye flour and then enough white flour to attain desired consistency. Mix until lump-free.

3. Beat egg whites until they form soft peaks. Gently mix into the batter.

4. Preheat waffle iron. Just before cooking, dissolve baking soda in 1 tablespoon warm water and gently blend into the batter.

5. Pour some of the batter onto waffle iron and cook for 7 to 8 minutes. Repeat with remaining batter. Serve hot.

Ham Waffles

Makes 3 waffles

Ham is another one of those savory ingredients that's a perfect partner for sourdough.

> 2 cups culture from the first proof (page 37)
>
> 2 eggs, separated
>
> 1 cup chopped ham
>
> ½ cup milk
>
> 2 tablespoons butter, melted
>
> 2 teaspoons sugar
>
> Several tablespoons white bread flour, if needed
>
> ½ teaspoon baking soda

SECOND PROOF AND BAKING

1. Measure the culture into a large mixing bowl. Add egg yolks, ham, milk, melted butter, and sugar to the culture and mix briefly.

2. Add flour to attain desired consistency. Mix until lump-free.

3. Beat egg whites until they form soft peaks, and gently mix into the batter.

4. Preheat waffle iron. Just before cooking, dissolve baking soda in 1 tablespoon warm water and gently blend into the batter.

5. Pour some of the batter onto waffle iron and cook for 7 to 8 minutes. Repeat with remaining batter. Serve hot.

Buttermilk Waffles

Makes 3 or 4 waffles

Buttermilk today is usually made from pasteurized skim milk to which a culture has been added to improve flavor and consistency. For a real treat, search out a country dairy and get the buttermilk that is a residue of butter churning.

2 cups culture from the first proof (page 37)

2 eggs, separated

$1/2$ cup buttermilk

2 tablespoons butter, melted

2 tablespoons sugar

1 teaspoon salt

White bread flour as needed (about $1/2$ to 1 cup)

SECOND PROOF AND BAKING

1. Measure the culture into a large mixing bowl. Add egg yolks, buttermilk, melted butter, sugar, and salt to the culture and mix briefly.

2. Add enough flour to attain the desired consistency. Mix until lump-free. Proof, covered, 1 hour at 85°.

3. Beat egg whites until they form soft peaks, and gently mix into the batter.

4. Preheat waffle iron. Pour batter onto waffle iron and cook for 7 to 8 minutes. Repeat with remaining batter. Serve hot.

Gingerbread Waffles

Makes 3 or 4 waffles

The flavor of ginger is unique in either bread or waffles. Unless you've tried both, you have missed a treat.

2 cups culture from the first proof (page 37)

2 eggs, separated

$1/2$ cup milk

2 tablespoons butter, melted

2 tablespoons molasses

2 tablespoons firmly packed brown sugar

1 teaspoon ground ginger

1 teaspoon ground cinnamon

1 teaspoon salt

White bread flour as needed ($1/2$ to 1 cup)

$1/2$ teaspoon baking soda

SECOND PROOF AND BAKING

1. Measure the culture into a large mixing bowl. Add egg yolks, milk, melted butter, molasses, brown sugar, ginger, cinnamon, and salt to the culture and mix briefly.

2. Add enough flour to attain the desired consistency. Mix until lump-free.

3. Beat egg whites until they form soft peaks, and gently mix into the batter.

4. Preheat waffle iron. Just before cooking, dissolve the baking soda in 1 tablespoon warm water and gently blend into batter.

5. Pour some of the batter onto waffle iron and cook for 7 to 8 minutes. Repeat with remaining batter. Serve hot.

Whole Wheat Waffles

Makes 3 or 4 waffles

You may need to use 1 cup of white flour to get the ideal waffle texture.

2 cups culture from the first proof (page 37)
2 eggs, separated
$^1/_2$ cup milk
2 tablespoons butter, melted
2 teaspoons sugar
1 teaspoon salt
$^1/_2$ cup whole wheat flour
White bread flour as needed
$^1/_2$ teaspoon baking soda

SECOND PROOF AND BAKING

1. Measure the culture into a large mixing bowl. Add egg yolks, milk, melted butter, sugar, and salt to the culture and mix briefly.

2. Add the whole wheat flour. Add enough white flour to attain the desired consistency. Mix until lump-free.

3. Beat egg whites until they form soft peaks, and gently mix into the batter.

4. Preheat waffle iron. Just before baking, dissolve the baking soda in 1 tablespoon warm water and gently blend into the batter.

5. Pour some of the batter onto waffle iron and cook for 7 to 8 minutes. Repeat with remaining batter. Serve hot.

Sour Cream Waffles

Makes 3 waffles

Does sour cream make sourdough more sour? Yes, but just a tad enhances the tang of sourdough.

> **2 cups culture from the first proof (page 37)**
> **2 eggs, separated**
> **1 cup sour cream**
> **2 teaspoons sugar**
> **1 teaspoon salt**
> **White bread flour as needed**
> **1/2 teaspoon baking soda**

SECOND PROOF AND BAKING

1. Measure the culture into a large mixing bowl. Add egg yolks, sour cream, sugar, and salt to the culture and mix briefly.

2. Add enough flour to attain desired consistency. Mix until lump-free.

3. Beat egg whites until they form soft peaks, and gently mix into the batter.

4. Preheat waffle iron. Just before cooking, dissolve baking soda in 1 tablespoon warm water and gently blend into the batter.

5. Pour some of the batter onto waffle iron and cook for 7 to 8 minutes. Repeat with remaining batter. Serve hot.

Blueberry Waffles

Makes 3 or 4 waffles

Use fresh blueberries if possible; frozen berries are a good second choice.

2 cups culture from the first proof (page 37)

1 cup fresh or frozen blueberries (thawed and drained, if frozen)

2 eggs, separated

2 tablespoons butter, melted

2 teaspoons sugar

1 teaspoon salt

White bread flour as needed

¹/₂ teaspoon baking soda

SECOND PROOF AND BAKING

1. Measure the culture into a large mixing bowl. Add blueberries, egg yolks, melted butter, sugar, and salt to the culture and mix briefly.

2. Add enough flour to attain the desired consistency. Mix until lump-free.

3. Beat egg whites until they form soft peaks, and gently mix into the batter.

4. Preheat waffle iron. Just before cooking, dissolve the baking soda in 1 tablespoon warm water and gently blend into the batter.

5. Pour some of the batter onto a preheated waffle iron and cook for 7 to 8 minutes. Repeat with remaining batter. Serve hot.

BATTER BREADS

Sourdough cultures are as successful with batter breads as with all other breads. Batters are lighter doughs that are mixed entirely by beating, either by hand or with an electric mixer. No kneading is involved. I give a basic recipe for sourdough batter that you can make using any culture. Each of the recipes in this section starts with this batter and then calls for adding special ingredients for a variety of breads. When adding special ingredients, it is best to mix them into the culture before adding the flour. The basic recipe below makes a good white batter bread.

Basic Sourdough Batter Bread

Makes 1 loaf

2 cups culture from the first proof (page 37)

2 tablespoons butter

$^1/_2$ cup milk

1 teaspoon salt

2 tablespoons sugar

3 cups white bread flour

SECOND PROOF AND BAKING

1. Measure the culture into a large mixing bowl. Melt the butter over moderate heat, add the milk to the butter and warm (to 75° to 85°). Add the salt and sugar and stir until dissolved. Add this mixture to the culture and mix well.

2. Add the flour, 1 cup at a time, mixing vigorously for 1 minute or so between cups. The yield is approximately 3^1/$_2$ cups of basic sourdough batter.

3. Grease a 4^1/$_2$ × 8^1/$_2$-inch loaf pan if not nonstick. Spoon batter into the prepared pan.

4. Proof, covered, at 85° for 1 to 2 hours, or until dough rises ^{1}/$_2$ inch above the edge of the pan.

5. Preheat oven to 350°. Bake for 45 minutes.

6. Remove loaf from pan and cool on a wire rack.

Banana Batter Bread

Makes 1 loaf

In addition to being easy, this combination of sourdough, bananas, and nuts results in a pleasing and unusual texture.

> **Sourdough batter (page 144)**
> **1 egg, beaten**
> **1 cup mashed banana**
> **^{1}/$_2$ cup sugar**
> **^{1}/$_2$ cup chopped nuts**

SECOND PROOF AND BAKING

1. Complete steps 1 and 2 to prepare sourdough batter. Add the egg, banana, sugar, and nuts to the batter and mix well.

2. Spoon the batter into a 4^1/$_2$ × 8^1/$_2$-inch loaf pan.

3. Proof, covered, at 85° for 1 to 2 hours, or until dough rises ^{1}/$_2$ inch above the edge of the pan.

4. Preheat oven to 350°. Bake for 45 minutes.

5. Remove from loaf pan and cool on a wire rack.

Cheese Batter Bread

Makes 1 loaf

Just a glance at the ingredients in this recipe is sure to convince you to give it a try.

> Sourdough batter (page 144)
> 2 teaspoons caraway seeds
> 1 cup grated cheese
> 1/2 teaspoon garlic powder
> 2 eggs, beaten

SECOND PROOF AND BAKING

1. Complete steps 1 and 2 to prepare sourdough batter. Add caraway seeds, cheese, garlic powder, and eggs to the batter and mix well.

2. Spoon the batter into a $4^{1}/_{2} \times 8^{1}/_{2}$-inch loaf pan.

3. Proof, covered, at 85° for 1 to 2 hours, or until dough rises 1/2 inch above the edge of the pan.

4. Preheat oven to 350°. Bake for 45 minutes.

5. Remove loaf from pan and cool on a wire rack.

Corn Batter Bread

Makes 1 loaf

This is not your standard cornbread! The sage, celery seed, and cornmeal give the sourdough base an earthy quality.

> Sourdough batter (page 144)
> 1 teaspoon ground sage
> 2 teaspoons celery seed
> 1/2 cup yellow cornmeal

SECOND PROOF AND BAKING

1. Complete steps 1 and 2 to prepare sourdough batter. Add the sage, celery seed, and corn meal to the batter and mix well.

2. Spoon the batter into a $4^{1}/_{2} \times 8^{1}/_{2}$-inch loaf pan.

3. Proof, covered, at 85° for 1 to 2 hours, or until dough rises $^{1}/_{2}$ inch above the edge of the pan.

4. Preheat oven to 350°. Bake for 45 minutes.

5. Remove loaf from pan and cool on a wire rack.

Dill Batter Bread

Makes 1 loaf

This bread is great for informal gatherings like an evening of card games, or for rainy day snacking.

> **Sourdough batter (page 144)**
> **1 cup grated Parmesan cheese**
> **$^{1}/_{2}$ cup chopped onions**
> **2 teaspoons dill seed**

SECOND PROOF AND BAKING

1. Complete steps 1 and 2 to prepare sourdough batter. Add cheese, onions, and dill seed to the batter and mix well.

2. Spoon the batter into a $4^{1}/_{2} \times 8^{1}/_{2}$-inch loaf pan.

3. Proof, covered, at 85° for 1 to 2 hours, or until dough rises $^{1}/_{2}$ inch above the edge of the pan.

4. Preheat oven to 350°. Bake for 45 minutes.

5. Remove loaf from pan and cool on a wire rack.

Limpa Batter Bread

Makes 1 loaf

Sourdough limpas, in any form, are wonderful. Of all the batter breads, this is probably my favorite.

> **Sourdough batter (page 144)**
> **2 tablespoons molasses**
> **1 teaspoon caraway seeds**
> **Grated rind of 1 orange**
> **1 cup rye flour**
> **$^1/_4$ cup milk**

SECOND PROOF AND BAKING

1. Complete steps 1 and 2 to prepare sourdough batter. Add the molasses, caraway seeds, orange rind, rye flour, and milk to the batter and mix well.

2. Spoon the batter into a $4^1/_2 \times 8^1/_2$-inch loaf pan.

3. Proof, covered, at 85° for 1 to 2 hours, or until dough rises $^1/_2$ inch above the edge of the pan.

4. Preheat oven to 350°. Bake for 45 minutes.

5. Remove loaf from pan and cool on a wire rack.

Nut Batter Bread

Makes 1 loaf

This has the flavor of cinnamon rolls and makes a more than interesting batter bread.

> **Sourdough batter (page 144)**
> **1 teaspoon each ground cinnamon and nutmeg**
> **1 cup raisins**
> **$^1/_2$ cup chopped nuts**

SECOND PROOF AND BAKING

1. Complete steps 1 and 2 to prepare sourdough batter. Add the cinnamon, nutmeg, raisins, and nuts to the batter and mix well.

2. Spoon the batter into a $4^1/_2 \times 8^1/_2$-inch loaf pan.

3. Proof, covered, at 85° for 1 to 2 hours, or until dough rises $^1/_2$ inch above the edge of the pan.

4. Preheat oven to 350°. Bake for 45 minutes.

5. Remove loaf from pan and cool on a wire rack.

Whole Wheat Batter Bread

Makes 1 loaf

This batter bread is heavier than most of the others and may take a long time to rise.

> **Sourdough batter (page 144)**
> **3 tablespoons molasses**
> **1 egg, beaten**
> **1 cup whole wheat flour**

SECOND PROOF AND BAKING

1. Complete steps 1 and 2 to prepare sourdough batter. Add the molasses, egg, and whole wheat flour to the batter and mix well.

2. Spoon the batter into a $4^1/_2 \times 8^1/_2$-inch loaf pan.

3. Proof, covered, at 85° for 1 to 2 hours, or until dough rises $^1/_2$ inch above the edge of the pan.

4. Preheat oven to 350°. Bake for 45 minutes.

5. Remove loaf from pan and cool on a wire rack.

CHAPTER 6

BAKING SOURDOUGHS IN BREAD MACHINES

MAKING SOURDOUGH BREAD IN a bread machine is not as simple as making other types of bread in a machine. The fermentation action by which lactobacilli produce the sourdough flavor still takes approximately 12 hours to complete with an active culture, regardless of whether the bread is being made by hand or by machine. The real problem in making sourdough bread in a bread machine is getting the dough to rise on schedule. When the "last rise" cycle starts, the wild yeast must be at their peak activity so that the loaf is leavened completely before baking begins.

The best proofing temperature for a sourdough culture is 85° to 95°. To achieve this temperature, you can place a proofing box (page 40) over your mixing bowls and even over the top of your bread machine, if needed, during the mixing and proofing cycles. Be sure to remove it before the bake cycle starts.

Culture Preparation

This step occurs before you place the ingredients in the bread machine. It reactivates the culture and gets it ready for use. (For how to activate and establish a culture, see pages 36–38.) The time this step takes is determined by how fast the yeast begin to multiply, which depends on the specific culture and on how long it has been refrigerated. If it is a fast culture (such as the Russian culture available from Sourdoughs International [page 176]) and is used weekly, it will be up to speed in 3 hours or less. If the culture hasn't been used for a month or so or is a slower type, it may take 6 to 8 hours or longer. You judge this by the activity in the culture after it is fed and warmed. Add 1 cup of flour and ³/₄ cup of water to the culture. (You can do this in the jar you use to store the culture, if there is room.) Mix well and put the culture in a warm place (85° to 95°) or proofing box. When a layer of bubbles forms (¹/₂ to 1 inch), the culture is ready for the next step, the first proof.

The First Proof

The first proof is the 12-hour period that allows the lactobacilli in the culture to produce the sourdough flavor. It can be done in or out of the bread machine. If it is done in a bowl outside the machine, mix together half of the flour and all of the culture specified by the recipe, along with sufficient water to maintain a thick, pancake-batter consistency. Cover the mixture with plastic wrap or a dry cloth and proof at 85° to 90° for 8 to 10 hours. How long you proof it depends on the length of time of your machine allows before baking starts. For example, if your machine utilizes 3 hours in the kneading, resting, and rising cycles, you would transfer the culture to the machine after 9 hours, add the remaining flour and other ingredients called for in the recipe, and turn it on. Then, with 3 hours in the machine, the lactobacilli will have their full 12 hours for flavor production.

If you prefer to do the first proof in the machine, add the flour and culture to the machine as just described, start the cycle, and mix for 10 minutes or so, then turn the machine off for 8 to 10 hours, again depending on the duration of your machine's cycle. After that time, add the remaining flour and other ingredients of the recipe and start the machine.

Regardless of whether you do the first proof in or out of the machine, you should focus on what is happening to the wild yeast as the lactobacilli are doing their thing. After 9 hours a fast yeast will have utilized the nutrients in the flour and become mildly dormant. If you are using a fast culture, adding the additional flour called for in the recipe will have the yeast back to its maximum activity in 1 to 2 hours, giving it just enough time to leaven the dough before baking starts. But if the culture is not working as quickly as it should, the dough may not leaven completely before baking starts. What to do? Almost all machines have a delay cycle. After the first proof, when you add the remaining ingredients, turn the machine on briefly to mix everything together. Then turn it off and program a delay for 1 hour or so. This should give a fast culture all the time it needs. You may have to experiment a bit to develop a schedule that works with your culture in your environment, but that is the way to start. The speed of a culture—that is, how long it takes to reach maximum activity—is obviously crucial to the machine baker. Later I describe how to determine the speed of your culture (page 154).

Actually achieving the timing you want on a specific machine may be a challenge. Virtually all machines can be programmed to allow a delay, which can be helpful but will not necessarily solve all the problems of short rising cycles, ill-timed "shakes," and inappropriate kneading cycles that are not necessary with sourdoughs. In general, it is desirable to select the cycle that will give you the longest last rise possible and to use a culture that can leaven within that time.

Bread Machine Features for Baking Real Sourdough

I am not quite so bold as Dan Leader, author of *Bread Alone*, who predicts, with some justification, that bread machines will end up on the garage shelf, but the manufacturers do have a lot to learn if their products are going to be useful with sourdough. However, I have successfully and consistently baked good sourdoughs in a variety of machines. At this time it does involve more art than science. No machine on the market is ideally designed for sourdoughs. A couple have programmable design features that are helpful, but even they seem poorly contrived. One allows the baker to set three variables in advance, allowing a total rising time of up to 170 minutes, which should be ideal for sourdoughs. Unfortunately, there is a shaping "shake" just before the second rise that is equivalent to punching the dough down. This results in a final rising of just 90 minutes. These shaping tremors occurs in many machines and create problems for sourdough bakers. One reader of the previous edition told me that he reaches into the dough and removes the paddle just as the first rise starts. Then when the shake occurs only the paddle rod revolves and the subsequent disturbance is far less traumatic. However, if the paddle is removed from some of the machines, a hole is exposed in the bottom of the pan which cannot be worked around. Some machines can simply be turned off for the duration of a cycle and turned on again later. However, turning off the power usually returns the process to the initial mixing cycle and repeats the entire program. One machine actually permits the user to set the timing for every cycle, but not in advance! To change from one cycle to another, the baker must stand by to press a control switch to start the next cycle. This is not all bad since the last rise can be extended indefinitely until the dough has risen as much as desired. (And with some slow sourdoughs that can be quite a while.) Then, if the results are satisfactory, that particular set of timed cycles can be stored in the machine's memory for future use. But the machines can only store one "menu." Bakers usually want to fine tune just one or two of the cycles, such as the final rise. The only way to do so is to monitor the entire process again. This is hardly the image of convenience that the bread machine industry projects. Most machines are programmable only to the extent of allowing one to select which type of bread is to be baked. The machine then sets the individual cycles for that type of bread.

In spite of these deficiencies, you can bake sourdoughs in almost any bread machine. Time permitting, however, the best way to use a bread machine for sourdoughs—any culture, any machine—is to use the dough cycle (page 154).

Dough Consistency

In addition to timing, correct dough consistency is critical for success with sourdoughs in a machine. This is a particular problem with sourdoughs, because one is never precisely sure how much flour and water is added with the culture. If the dough is too thin, it will often rise well and then collapse. If it is too thick, it may not rise as well. The problem is fairly easy to correct, providing you recognize it at the start and add either a little additional water or flour, whichever is indicated.

The trick is to recognize the problem in time to correct it; this is done by watching the kneading paddle after you've added the remaining flour and recipe ingredients. After the dough has been kneading for 3 to 4 minutes and all the ingredients are well mixed, the dough should form a soft ball that catches and drags on the sides and bottom of the pan as the paddle revolves. If instead it forms a firm ball that revolves with or on the paddle and doesn't catch on the sides, it is too thick and isn't kneading properly at all. To correct this, add water, 1 tablespoon at a time, until the dough begins to adhere. If the dough doesn't form a ball, it is too thin. To correct this, add flour, 1 tablespoon at a time. Allow sufficient time after adding either flour or water for it to be incorporated into the dough before adding more. Most machines have two kneading cycles, and you should check the consistency on both cycles.

Some machines have a rod that projects from the sides of the pan and catches the dough as it revolves. This, I believe, provides a superior kneading action. Others have a paddle and pan configuration that produces a peculiar formation in the kneading dough that resembles a miniature tornado as it curls and twists up the sides of the pan. This produces a good kneading action and indicates that the consistency is excellent. Judging paddle consistency takes experience with the machine you are using, since there is considerable variation in the size, shape, and ridges in the pan wall, all affecting the efficiency of the kneading action.

Determining a Culture's Peak Leavening Rate

It is essential to know the peak leavening rate for every culture that you use; if you markedly increase or decrease the frequency with which you use a culture, it is desirable to repeat the process. Fortunately, it is easy to do. Remove the culture from the refrigerator, feed it 1 cup flour and $3/4$ cup warm water, mix well, and place it in a proofing box or other warm place for 5 to 6 hours, until it appears active. Next, adjust the level of the culture in the jar to slightly less than half full, and add $1/2$ cup each of flour and warm water. Mix well. Then observe the jar at approximately hourly intervals. When the foam level reaches its maximum height, it is at its peak of activity. When it begins to recede, the peak is over. An aggressive Russian culture (such as the one available from Sourdoughs International [page 176]) will reach the top of the jar in less than 3 hours. A slow culture may never produce a foam layer more than 1 or 2 inches thick, but when it does, it has also reached its peak of activity.

The Dough Cycle

The bread machine has been promoted as the answer to simplified baking for the person with limited time who wants to program the machine to deliver fresh-baked bread at breakfast with only 5 or 10 minutes of effort. And, granted, it does a fair job of doing just that. With a little attention, it will even do a reasonable job with sourdoughs. But if you expect really superb sourdough, the kind that your friends and relatives will compare with that loaf they tasted in San Francisco, you've got to use the dough cycle.

At best, sourdough baked in a home machine will taste like sourdough, but it will never have that chewy thick crust. And it will look like either a pressed fireplace log or a 4 × 4 timber, instead of an intriguing French loaf with a slashed crust. The machine will never bake an Arab pita bread, a Swiss braid, a Russian round, or a pan of dinner rolls. But you can do all of that with the dough cycle, and it's easier than you think!

The exciting part is that you can use any culture, regardless of its leavening speed, and almost any machine, regardless of its idiosyncrasies, and you can expect to have better sourdoughs than you can buy anywhere.

First, complete the culture preparation and the first proof, as described on pages 150 to 152. Then add the remaining flour and other ingredients to complete the recipe, turn the machine on, and set it to the dough cycle. It will automatically turn off before the baking cycle starts—in about 2 hours, depending on the machine. Removing the dough is relatively simple if your hands are well floured. Transfer it to a floured board; now the real pleasure of baking begins. This dough is usually somewhat moister than dough produced by hand and you may have to knead in a little additional flour. Now you can shape the dough in any way you like. Refer elsewhere in this book for instructions on forming and baking loaves, braids, pita breads, or any bread you desire.

Because bread machines come in several sizes, the following recipes give instructions for making medium (1½-pound) and large (2-pound) loaves. It would be disasterous to use the large-loaf instructions for a machine of smaller capacity, but you can use the medium-loaf instructions with larger machines—just don't expect the loaves to rise to the top of the bread pan.

World Bread

Makes 1 loaf

This is a universal and basic white bread available around the world. It has probably been baked with all known sourdough cultures, as well as those now "extinct." With a fast culture, you can bake this recipe on the white or standard bread cycle (60 to 75 minutes). With a slow culture, you should use the French bread cycle, which has a longer final rise (120 minutes) before baking.

	MEDIUM	LARGE
Prepared sourdough culture (page 150)	1 1/2 cups	2 1/2 cups
Warm milk (75° to 85°)	1/4 cup	1/3 cup
Salt	3/4 teaspoon	1 teaspoon
Sugar	1 tablespoon	2 tablespoons
Vegetable oil	2 teaspoons	2 tablespoons
White bread flour	2 cups	3 cups
Water or flour as needed to adjust consistency		

1. Mix the culture and half of the flour in the machine for 5 to 10 minutes. Turn the machine off for 8 hours.

2. Mix the milk, salt, sugar, and vegetable oil together by hand briefly; add to the culture and mix briefly by machine.

3. Set the machine to the white bread or French bread cycle and start the initial knead while adding the remaining flour.

4. Adjust the consistency with additional water or flour 1 tablespoon at a time, and check the paddle action (page 153).

Light Swedish Limpa Bread

Makes 1 loaf

Limpas are rye breads with brown sugar or molasses. The orange zest should be coarsely grated. The addition of gluten produces a lighter bread in a 90- to 120-minute final rise with a fast culture.

	MEDIUM	LARGE
Prepared sourdough culture (page 150)	1 1/2 cups	3 cups
White bread flour	1 1/2 cups	3 cups
Water	1/4 cup	1/2 cup
Vegetable oil	2 teaspoons	1 tablespoon
Firmly packed brown sugar	1/4 cup	1/3 cup
Grated orange zest	1/2 orange	1 orange
Salt	1/2 teaspoon	1 teaspoon
Gluten flour	1 1/2 teaspoons	2 teaspoons
Caraway seeds	2 teaspoons	1 tablespoon
Fennel seeds	2 teaspoons	1 tablespoon
Medium rye flour	1/2 cup	3/4 cup
Water or flour as needed to adjust consistency		

1. Mix the culture and half of the white flour in the machine for 5 to 10 minutes. Turn the machine off for 8 hours.

2. Add the water, vegetable oil, and brown sugar to the culture mixture in the machine and mix for 5 minutes. Add the remaining white flour and mix for 5 minutes.

3. Add the orange zest, salt, gluten, and caraway and fennel seeds to the rye flour and mix briefly by hand. Add this to the mixture in the machine and knead 10 minutes.

4. Add water or white flour, 1 tablespoon at a time, to adjust the consistency as needed.

5. Set the machine to French bread or any cycle that has a 90-minute last rise before baking.

Tanya's Peasant Black Bread

Makes 1 loaf

Every baker should try this. The heavy dough requires a fast culture in the average machine cycle. Be sure your culture will be at its peak of activity just as the last rise starts. It should be successful in a programmable machine with 120 minutes for that last rise before baking. The heavy rye and whole wheat flours require the gluten flour. The coriander and molasses complement the sourdough flavors.

	MEDIUM	LARGE
Prepared sourdough culture (page 150)	1 1/3 cups	3 cups
White bread flour	1 cup	2 cups
Salt	1/2 teaspoon	1 teaspoon
Sugar	1 tablespoon	2 tablespoons
Warm milk (75° to 85°)	1/4 cup	1/2 cup
Dark molasses	1 tablespoon	2 tablespoons
Ground coriander	1 teaspoon	1 1/2 teaspoons
Vital gluten	2 teaspoons	1 tablespoon
Rye flour	1/2 cup	1 cup
Whole wheat flour	1/2 cup	1 cup
Water or flour as needed to adjust consistency		

1. Mix the culture and half of the white flour in the machine for 5 to 10 minutes. Turn the machine off for 8 hours.

2. Dissolve the salt and sugar in the warm milk by stirring briefly. Add it to the machine with the molasses and coriander. Mix 5 minutes.

3. Combine the gluten, rye flour, whole wheat flour, and remaining white flour by hand and add to the machine.

4. Set the machine to French bread and start the initial knead while adding water or flour, 1 tablespoon at a time, until paddle consistency is satisfactory (page 153).

Anise Rye Bread

Makes 1 loaf

Anise and rye blend surprisingly well with sourdough in this unusual recipe.

	MEDIUM	LARGE
Prepared sourdough culture (page 150)	1½ cups	3 cups
White bread flour	1½ cups	3 cups
Water	¼ cup	½ cup
Salt	½ teaspoon	1 teaspoon
Sugar	2 teaspoons	1 tablespoon
Ground anise	½ teaspoon	1 teaspoon
Vegetable oil	1 tablespoon	2 tablespoons
Vital gluten	1 teaspoon	2 teaspoons
Rye flour	½ cup	1 cup
Water or flour as needed to adjust consistency		

1. Mix the culture and half of the white flour in the machine for 5 to 10 minutes. Turn the machine off for 8 hours.

2. Add the water, salt, sugar, anise, and vegetable oil to the culture and mix for 5 minutes.

3. Blend gluten and rye flour by hand and add, with the remaining white flour, to the culture mixture.

4. Start the French bread cycle.

5. Adjust the consistency with additional water or flour, 1 tablespoon at a time, checking the paddle action (page 153).

Caraway Rye Bread

Makes 1 loaf

Rye, caraway, and sourdough is a wonderful combination. This somewhat heavy dough does better with the addition of gluten flour. The slower Austrian culture used to test this recipe needs a 1-hour delay before the machine is started. (This culture is available from Sourdoughs International, page 173.)

	MEDIUM	LARGE
Prepared sourdough culture (page 150)	1¹/₂ cups	3 cups
White bread flour	1¹/₂ cups	3 cups
Water	¹/₄ cup	¹/₂ cup
Salt	¹/₂ teaspoon	1 teaspoon
Caraway seeds	2 teaspoons	1 tablespoon
Gluten flour	1 teaspoon	2 teaspoons
Rye flour	¹/₂ cup	1 cup
Water or flour as needed to adjust consistency		

1. Mix the culture and half of the white flour in the machine for 10 to 15 minutes. Turn the machine off for 8 hours.

2. Add the water, salt, and caraway seeds and mix 5 minutes.

3. Mix the gluten flour with the rye flour briefly by hand. Add it to the culture mixture in the machine and mix 10 minutes.

4. Add the remaining white flour and start the French bread cycle.

5. Adjust the consistency with additional water or flour, 1 tablespoon at a time, checking the paddle action (page 153).

Cheese Onion Bread

Makes 1 loaf

This is a real challenge to bake, but learning the secret is well worth the effort. Both the cheese and onions add moisture. During the initial kneading, the dough appears far too stiff. As kneading and resting occur, moisture will be drawn from the onions and the cheese will begin to melt. Thus, the true consistency becomes apparent later than with other recipes. When the second knead is in progress, evaluate the paddle consistency, and cautiously add water as indicated. It may be necessary to mix the onions and cheese into the culture in step 2 by hand. I do this by turning off the machine and using a rubber spatula to break up the ingredients; then I restart the machine.

	MEDIUM	LARGE
Prepared sourdough culture (page 150)	1 1/2 cups	3 cups
White bread flour	2 cups	3 1/2 cups
Chopped onion	1/4 cup	1/2 cup
Grated cheese	1/4 cup	1/2 cup
Vegetable oil	2 teaspoons	1 tablespoon
Salt	1/2 teaspoon	1 teaspoon
Water or flour as needed to adjust consistency		

1. Mix the culture and half of the flour in the machine for 5 to 10 minutes. Turn the machine off for 8 hours.

2. Add the onion, cheese, vegetable oil, and salt to the culture and mix 5 minutes.

3. Add the remaining flour and start the French bread cycle.

4. Adjust the consistency with additional water or flour, 1 tablespoon at a time, checking the paddle action (page 153).

Saudi Date Bread

Makes 1 loaf

I was concerned that the heavy load of dates and nuts in this recipe would weight down the dough, but it rose beautifully and held its structure when I tried it. The loaf weighed 2½ pounds! If you need a longer final rise, try using the dough cycle and a pan loaf that can rise as long as needed. I added the dates and nuts in Step 2, so that the somewhat heavy ingredients are better distributed throughout the bread. (The paddle action does not break them up.)

	MEDIUM	LARGE
Prepared sourdough culture (page 150)	1½ cups	3 cups
White bread flour	2 cups	4 cups
Sugar	1 tablespoon	2 tablespoons
Water	¼ cup	½ cup
Salt	½ teaspoon	1 teaspoon
Olive oil	2 teaspoons	1 tablespoon
Chopped dates	½ cup	1 cup
Chopped walnuts	½ cup	1 cup
Water or flour as needed to adjust consistency		

1. Mix the culture and half of the flour in the machine for 5 to 10 minutes. Turn the machine off for 8 hours.

2. Add the sugar, water, salt, olive oil, dates, and nuts to the culture and mix 5 minutes.

3. Add the remaining flour to the culture mixture.

4. Start the regular or French bread cycle.

5. Adjust the consistency with additional water or flour, 1 tablespoon at a time, checking the paddle action (page 153).

Oatmeal Bread

Makes 1 loaf

The rolled oats increase the fiber content of this white bread. I used our San Francisco culture (available from Sourdoughs International [page 178]) and scheduled a 1-hour delay before starting the French bread cycle. I like old-fashioned rolled oats in this recipe, but you can probably substitute the quick-cooking types as well.

	MEDIUM	LARGE
Prepared sourdough culture (page 150)	1 1/2 cups	3 cups
White bread flour	1 1/2 cups	3 cups
Water	2 tablespoons	3 tablespoons
Salt	1/2 teaspoon	1 teaspoon
Firmly packed brown sugar	1 tablespoon	2 tablespoons
Rolled oats	1 cup	1 1/2 cups
Water or flour as needed to adjust consistency		

1. Mix the culture and half of the flour in the machine for 5 to 10 minutes. Turn the machine off for 8 hours.

2. Add the water, salt, brown sugar, and rolled oats and mix for 5 minutes.

3. Add the remaining flour and start the French bread cycle.

4. Adjust the consistency with additional water or flour, 1 tablespoon at a time, checking the paddle action (page 153).

Sour Cream Rye Bread

Makes 1 loaf

This Austrian recipe is a great combination of flavors and is easy to make in any machine.

	MEDIUM	LARGE
Prepared sourdough culture (page 150)	1¹/2 cups	3 cups
White bread flour	1 cup	2 cups
Salt	1/2 teaspoon	1 teaspoon
Sugar	1¹/2 tablespoons	2 tablespoons
Vegetable oil	2 teaspoons	1 tablespoon
Sour cream	1/2 cup	1 cup
Caraway seeds	1 tablespoon	2 tablespoons
Gluten flour	2 teaspoons	1 tablespoon
Rye flour	1 cup	2 cups
Water or flour as needed to adjust consistency		

1. Mix the culture and half of the white flour in the machine for 5 to 10 minutes. Turn the machine off for 8 hours.

2. Add the salt, sugar, vegetable oil, sour cream, and caraway seeds to the culture and mix for 5 minutes.

3. Blend the gluten flour briefly with the rye flour by hand and add, with the remaining white flour, to the culture mixture.

4. Start the French bread cycle.

5. Adjust the consistency with additional water or flour, 1 tablespoon at a time, checking the paddle action (page 153).

Sunflower Bread

Makes 1 loaf

This recipe produces a light-textured, dark, nutty bread. Use raw sunflower seeds, not roasted, for best results. We tested it in several machines with last rises of between 75 and 90 minutes.

	MEDIUM	LARGE
Prepared sourdough culture (page 150)	1 1/2 cups	3 cups
White bread flour	1 cup	1 1/2 cups
Milk	1/4 cup	1/2 cup
Salt	1/2 teaspoon	1 teaspoon
Sugar	1 tablespoon	2 tablespoons
Butter, melted	1 tablespoon	2 tablespoons
Raw sunflower seeds	1/2 cup	1 cup
Gluten flour	2 teaspoons	1 tablespoon
Whole wheat flour	1 cup	1 1/2 cups
Water or flour as needed to adjust consistency		

1. Mix the culture and half of the white flour in the machine for 5 to 10 minutes. Turn the machine off for 8 hours.

2. Add the milk, salt, sugar, butter, and sunflower seeds to the culture and mix for 10 minutes.

3. Blend the gluten flour by hand briefly with the whole wheat flour and add, with the remaining white flour, to the culture mixture.

4. Start the French bread cycle.

5. Adjust the consistency with additional water or flour, 1 tablespoon at a time, checking the paddle action (page 153).

Sunflower Spelt Bread

Makes 1 loaf

Purity Foods cautions that spelt gluten is much more fragile than the glutens of other wheats. Thus, mixing times should be dramatically reduced to ensure optimum loaf volume. I do not believe this is a significant problem with hand mixing, but in a machine it could be. In my test baking with spelt, I did the initial mixing by hand, and the first proof took place in a bowl separate from the machine. At the end of the first proof, I added the remaining ingredients, mixed the dough briefly by hand, and then added the mixture to the machine, where I limited kneading to 10 minutes while I adjusted the dough's consistency. The bread rose very well. We probably have a lot to learn about using spelt flour in a bread machine, but these cautions should be helpful.

	MEDIUM	LARGE
Prepared sourdough culture (page 150)	1 ½ cups	3 cups
White spelt flour	1 cup	2 cups
Milk	¼ cup	½ cup
Salt	1 teaspoon	2 teaspoons
Sugar	1 tablespoon	2 tablespoons
Vegetable oil or melted butter	1 tablespoon	2 tablespoons
Raw sunflower seeds	½ cup	1 cup
Whole spelt flour	1 cup	2 cups
Water or flour as needed to adjust consistency		

1. Mix the culture and half of the white spelt flour in the machine for 5 to 10 minutes. Turn the machine off for 8 hours.

2. Add the milk, salt, sugar, oil, and sunflower seeds to the culture and mix for 10 minutes.

3. Add the whole spelt flour and the remaining white spelt flour to the culture mixture.

4. Start the French bread cycle.

5. Adjust the consistency with additional water or flour, 1 tablespoon at a time, checking the paddle action (page 153).

CHAPTER 7

WILD CULTURES FROM SOURDOUGHS INTERNATIONAL

WHEN I RETURNED FROM THE Middle East with a refrigerator full of wild sourdough cultures, I was reminded of their vitality every time I opened the refrigerator and saw them bubbling at me. I wondered, if anyone was as enchanted by those cultures as much as I was. How to find out? I couldn't imagine sending those fermenting mixtures through the mail. Instead, I experimented with drying them and then adding water to reconstitute the mixture. They survived the drying, but when I poured a sourdough culture on a baking sheet and let it dry, it formed a rock hard sheet that was almost impossible to break, grind, or mix with water. It took months of testing, but by carefully regulating the drying temperature and adding flour at the right moment I managed to encapsulate the delicate yeasts in a cocoon of flour that dissolves easily in water and starts them off to bake for another century or so.

What do you name a company that grows and sells wild sourdough cultures? Ed's Breads didn't quite do it. My most creative thinking usually occurs about 2 A.M. and that's when Sourdoughs International popped in and stayed.

With a company name, a book, and eight priceless wild sourdough cultures, we were off and running (running scared, that is). I thought it would be a great challenge and a lot of fun to market and distribute the book and cultures. There was just one problem. I hated sales. I shall never forget that first sales call I made, knocking timidly on the office door of the owner of Boise's Book Shop. She was busy and I was an interruption. I left with an order for 10 books, a warm glow, and the memory of a very gracious lady. Since then I've met thousands of people throughout the world who are as committed to the rebirth and preservation of sourdoughs as I am.

Along the way I acquired two additional cultures, one from Russia and the latest from Finland, and I expect to add more to our offerings in the years ahead. There has been marvelous media coverage from food writers coast to coast who have assisted us enormously in our modest success. We are still largely a mail-order business. With today's communication technology—a toll-free number, a fax, and an Internet home page—selling ancient sourdough cultures is stream-lined. That certainly qualifies as an oxymoron. (Ordering information is on page 178.) You must join me and other dedicated bakers who are already enjoying the world's best bread.

Our World Cultures

Is one sourdough really different from another? Of course! They differ in flavor, sourness, and speed and strength of leavening. The true purist judges sourdoughs based primarily on their flavor, and then on their sourness. Evaluating the flavors of sourdough breads is not quite as complicated as wine tasting (there are no "stemmy" sourdoughs) but it may be close. I suspect that most of us have eaten enough commercial "sourdough" with its additives of vinegar and acetic acid to believe it should all taste that sour. It really isn't so. Having said that, I should acknowledge that on rare occasion a customer will complain that one of our cultures is too sour.

Breads of the Middle East

In many parts of the Middle East, bread baking is virtually unchanged from its inception ten thousand years ago. These ancient bakeries are as likely to be found in the middle of metropolitan Cairo as in the smallest and most remote desert village. They are usually secluded on village streets in thick mud-walled buildings that conceal ovens developed eons ago. And it is very difficult to gain entry. The proprietors are suspicious of any non-Arab seeking information. The language barrier adds to the difficulty, but even with a native guide we faced rebuff at every turn.

It was in this environment that we sought and found our sourdough cultures from antiquity. Gaining access was an achievement, leaving with a sample of unbaked dough a triumph. Tact, diplomacy, sign language, pantomime, and a smile sometimes accomplished what often seemed beyond reach. Getting those precious samples of dried, unidentifiable white substances through airports and multiple custom inspections was the culmination of each adventure. From our successes we selected four cultures to represent the Middle East. Two are from Egypt, the acknowledged home of humankind's first bakery; one is from Bahrain, the ancient Garden of Eden and an early crossroads of trade routes between the East, the Middle East, and Europe; and one is from Saudi Arabia, because no collection of breads from the Middle East would be complete without a sourdough culture from the desert kingdom.

THE GIZA SOURDOUGH

I believe the Giza culture is very likely the oldest one we offer. It comes from the rich Nile agricultural area isolated for centuries by a desert on one side and the Red Sea on the other—the ideal circumstances to protect a culture from contamination. It has a moderate to slow leavening speed with a mild flavor and moderate sourness. It is not suitable for bread machines except when using a dough cycle. It is an excellent culture for flatbreads and pitas.

We met Hamid, a gregarious taxi driver, in Cairo. He spoke English and claimed to have spent four years driving a cab in New York City. Driving in Cairo is an incredible experience. With a population of sixteen million, there seems to be a car for every person and absolutely no place to drive, park, or dodge. Hamid did all those things while talking and looking us straight in the eye as he barreled from one destination to another.

It took a while to convince Hamid that we wanted to go to an old bakery, not a new one, and we didn't want to buy bread at all. We wanted to visit and tour and talk to bakers. And we wanted some dough. Not bread, but dough. And we wanted to do it all in Giza. So off we went, with Hamid looking us in the eye and explaining that what we wanted might not be too easy. Egyptian bakers, he said, are not eager to have visitors, especially in the old bakeries we wanted to see. And because of increasing efforts to improve the sanitation of all food establishments, taking pictures and asking questions in an old bakery might intimidate them. Con artist that Hamid was, he was unable to get us past the front door of the first and second bakeries. Finally, it was my wife who got us into what looked like the oldest bakery in Giza, situated almost between the paws of the Sphinx.

There was a goat actually tied in the doorway. She made friends with it first. A ten-year-old boy, who was obviously very attached to the goat, was her next conquest. He worked in the bakery and was apparently the son of the proprietor. Did the lady want to come in? He could arrange it. With our youthful guide, we cautiously explored that ancient bakery. There were three small, dingy rooms. The dough, a mixture of flour, water, and the previous day's culture, was mixed in one room. The flatbreads were formed in another, and the oven was in the third. The hand-turned mixer was the only mechanical equipment. As the dough came from the mixer, it was pummeled by a baker until its consistency met his satisfaction. Round flatbreads about 10 inches in diameter were formed by hand and allowed to "rest" for 30 to 60 minutes. They were then placed on a very long paddle, thrust into the oven, and, with a quick twist, deposited on the oven's hot floor. Within a minute, they suddenly puffed violently, broke into a brief flash of flame, and, after another minute, were removed with a deft maneuver of the paddle. The bread was sold at the door as fast as it came from the oven. We could have purchased bread with the crowd at the door without difficulty. When Hamid explained that it was dough we really wanted, the owner needed an explanation. What was said is uncertain, but from the smiles and raised eyebrows, I suspect our sanity was being discussed. At any rate, we received a plastic bag of dough—and a flat bread—with the compliments of the owner.

THE RED SEA SOURDOUGH

When we found this culture in 1984, Hurghada on the Red Sea existed almost as it did in ancient times and so did the sourdough we discovered there. The Hurghada we saw no longer exists today. In its place are high-rise buildings, condominiums, resort hotels, and commercial yeast. This is one of our faster leavening cultures, suitable for most bread machines. It has a mild flavor and sourness. It works well for any bread recipe made by hand.

Hurghada proved to be everything we had hoped. Narrow, winding streets; thick, squat, mud-walled buildings; shuttered windows; Moslem dress. The streets were dotted with small shops selling vegetables, incense, and crafts. It was all *ancient* Egypt. We finally identified the town bakery by the rows of bread loaves spread on the street to rise in the hot afternoon sun. *"Men kam?"* (how much?) I asked, pointing to a stack of fresh-baked breads. *"Ashra"* came the answer. The negotiation completed, I bit into the bread. Hmmm, *"kuais"* (good). Then I was stuck. I had almost exhausted my limited supply of Arabic. How to ask for some unbaked dough? I tried a smile and a gesture. No response. Then I lifted my camera and pantomimed taking a picture. The reaction was immediate and emphatic: "*la, la*" (no, no). Suddenly, I was not only unwelcome, I was being asked to leave, and in no uncertain terms. At that moment, someone in the crowd stepped forward. "Can I help you?" came in welcome English. I explained my desire to obtain some unbaked dough, and he passed the words on to the proprietor, who anxiously eyed the gathering crowd, assessing his next move. He paused, then motioned me forward. The crisis was over and we entered another scene from Egypt's ancient past. The interior was dark and composed of many small, thick-walled rooms, lighted only from small, high windows. Each room was designated for a specific function. In one, flour and water were mixed in what looked like a cement mixer turned by hand. A 5-gallon bucket of "starter" from the previous day was added. That was the dough. Neither salt nor sugar was used. The dough was then divided among several rooms, and, depending on the room it went to, shaped into loaves, flatbreads, or rolls. Some loaves were allowed to rise, others were baked unleavened. The "production lines" flowed toward a large clay oven. We admired everything and the owner beamed with pride. I doubt that he ever understood our interest in his dough, but when asked, although obviously puzzled, he filled our small plastic bags.

Bahrain—Sourdough from the Garden of Eden

The Bahrain culture is one of our more inherently sour cultures. Remember that all sourdoughs will become more sour if proofing times are increased. The caveat is that the Bahrain will be somewhat more sour whether the proofing time is short or long. It is slow leavening and unsuitable for bread machines except those with a dough cycle. It is suitable for all bread recipes made by hand.

The history of Dilmun-Bahrain abounds with myths and names from antiquity: the Assyrian Empire, the Babylonians, Persia, Alexander the Great. It was known as the place of immortality, the Garden of Eden. Bahrain's strategic location and unusual water supply made it a center of trade more than four thousand years ago. Today, it is an archipelago of thirty-three islands located approximately halfway down the Gulf of Arabia. The name means "two seas," in reference to the many freshwater springs that arise offshore and on the islands.

The old Bahrain bakeries make flatbreads almost exclusively. The ovens are dome shaped and heated with wood. The baker places the uncooked flatbread on a cushion rounded to match the inside curve of the oven dome. With a deft move, he slaps the bread on the hot, inner surface of the oven. It glows and puffs briefly and the baker then expertly removes it.

We were met in Bahrain bakeries with the same suspicion that we experienced throughout the Middle East. As long as negotiations were confined to buying bread, visitors were tolerated, but any attempt to go further was resisted or refused outright. Most Western tourists in Bahrain buy food in the security of hotels, where they have more confidence in the integrity of the water and cuisine. Our inquiries at ancient bakeries immediately caused suspicion.

We were refused permission to enter bakeries several times, but finally, relying on basic Arab courtesy and the inherent curiosity of children, we succeeded. My wife struck up a smiling contest with a handsome youngster and offered his parent, who happened to work in an adjacent bakery, a Polaroid picture. We exchanged pleasantries and eventually gained access.

Although our presence in this bakery was tolerated grudgingly, we had no difficulty getting some unbaked dough. They surely thought our tastes peculiar, but from an ancient bakery in the land of Dilmun we acquired a bit of immortal history that may date into the distant past.

THE SAUDI ARABIAN SOURDOUGH

If you want to taste a sourdough with a different flavor, this is the one. It leavens at a moderate rate, is not generally suited to bread machines for that reason, and produces an absolutely out-of-this-world Arab pita bread. The best I've ever experienced.

Saudi Arabia is a rapidly changing country that has advanced two thousand years in one lifetime. For this reason, there is a surprising mixture of the old with the new. Most bedouins live now as they have always lived, in tents in the desert, tending their camels and goats. Even modern city dwellers retain much of the culture of the past.

The breads of the desert are the same today as they were hundreds of years ago. The bedouin sourdough cultures fed Mohammed, Lawrence of Arabia, and King Abdul Aziz. This was the culture we wanted for our desert breads. But where to find a bakery in the desert? The hospital I worked for was built 15 miles from

Riyadh to supply modern medical care to the Saudi Arabian National Guard and their families. The Guard, all desert Arabs, or bedouins, is charged with protecting the king and his family. They settled near the hospital and brought with them bedouin shops and souks. One was a bakery, producing a flatbread straight from the desert. This bakery, not half a mile from the hospital, in a solitary, dilapidated building beside the road, was best known for its spit-roasted chicken. It was irreverently known as "Chicken Charlie's," and it took us a year to realize that desert sourdough had searched us out, instead of us finding it.

Breads of Europe

The origin of Western civilization was somewhere in the Middle East, and the production of grains evolved in those areas and gradually spread northward to Europe. For hundreds of years, however, the dominant grain in Europe was rye, not wheat. In much of the developing world, rye was regarded as a weed, but in Europe it literally supplied the staff of life. As a result, recipes from the Germanic lands are heavily endowed with rye flavor.

Most sourdough cultures do not readily ferment rye flours. The amino acids and carbohydrates of the "weed" apparently require a special and hardy yeast. For this reason, we were especially pleased to find a sourdough culture that had obviously adapted to this task in the Austrian town of Innsbruck.

THE AUSTRIAN SOURDOUGH

This is the sourdough that almost changed my life, and I have some regrets about that. I'll bet the thirty years I could have served in a Saudi jail for its possession would have been material for a best-seller. The Innsbruck culture evolved in Austria. This culture doesn't leaven very rapidly. In some programmable machines you can usually maximize the last rising cycle and get by with a fairly heavy rye recipe. I recommend the culture for any recipe containing rye flour if made by hand.

We were on our way to Oberkochen in West Germany, where I was to learn to operate an electron microscope. On our way we took a detour through the lovely, medieval town of Innsbruck. By pure serendipity, we found ourselves staring through a bakery window with a sign proclaiming "sauerbraten"! The women tending the counter spoke not a word of English and we hardly a word of German. Hand signals worked wonders, and we pantomimed our way to a partially underground room where three bakers were preparing the day's bread. One spoke enough English to confirm that, indeed, they saved a portion of the dough each day to start the next day's mix. Without even looking, we had found a classic European sourdough. I dried the Innsbruck culture and wrapped it in aluminum foil.

Never in my worst dreams could I have imagined what would happen when I tried to take it back to Saudi Arabia. All was well until we got to Jeddah on our way back to Riyadh. You have to go through Saudi customs to believe what happens in this process. Your luggage is searched for contraband, including alcohol, drugs, and pornography (which might include a package of panty hose with a picture of women's legs). The metal detectors are set to be extremely sensitive. There is no mistaking the seriousness of the occasion. Violate a Saudi law and they may put you in jail and throw away the key. At the very least, you could be detained for twelve or more hours at the airport. The consequences are multiplied by the indifference of the foreign embassies.

I tripped one of the metal detectors and knew instantly that I was in serious trouble. The armed Saudi guard was taking no chances, and I was fast running out of ideas. How do you explain a packet of white, granular material to an airport security guard in a country where drug smuggling is so serious it doesn't even occur, especially when he doesn't understand your language and you don't understand his? Instantly a young guard motioned me to step aside and empty my pockets. I knew, without a doubt, that my aluminum foil packet of sourdough was the culprit, but I emptied my pockets of everything metal, hoping I could get under the detection level of the instrument. It didn't work. I tripped it again and again. By now I had the guard's full attention. What had looked at first like a routine pocket of change now required an explanation. The expression on my face didn't help as I tried to unscramble my brains and come up with an explanation. I finally tried, "Oh, maybe it's my lunch wrapper," and fished out what remotely resembled a very dry piece of bread wrapped in foil. I had no idea how much he understood of what I said. At that moment Allah must have smiled: some unlucky soul behind me tripped the detector. The guard glared at the interruption, made a quick decision, and motioned for me to pick up my possessions and go. I fled! Needless to say, I have never wrapped anything else in aluminum foil if there is a metal detector in my future.

THE FRENCH SOURDOUGH

Most of us are unaware that authentic sourdoughs in France are almost extinct. French bakers lost no time in converting to commercial yeast, and the real stuff has been hard to find for years with a few notable exceptions, perhaps Lionel Poilâne being the outstanding example. This culture leavens well, but not quickly, has a good flavor, is not overly sour, and does better when the bread is made by hand than in a machine. It works very well with the French Sourdough recipe.

No collection of European cultures would be complete without a representative from France, where bread has been an important factor in politics and survival since the French Revolution. While not as ancient as the breads of the Middle East, sourdough breads have sustained the French people since the Dark Ages. The very term "French bread" conjures an image of a sourdough bread familiar throughout most of the world.

The French are so possessive of their sourdough that we felt we had acquired a national treasure when we finally obtained a culture. Everyone in France seems absolutely convinced that there is only one French sourdough and is equally determined that it is not going to emigrate to the United States. We explained our mission to our taxi driver and told him about our collection of cultures from the Middle East. He was entranced. For a small, undetermined fee he would introduce us to a baker, his uncle. He brought the car to a screeching stop in front of a sidewalk cafe that was attached to an unimposing bakery. We took a table for four and ordered wine and bread. It wasn't long before the taxi driver returned with his gray-haired, portly uncle, the personification of a French baker. Another bottle of wine appeared. "And what do you think of the sourdough you are enjoying with the wine?" he asked. When we left two hours later, we had the French sourdough culture.

THE FINNISH SOURDOUGH

This is our newest culture. I've been using it for only two years. It is not a fast leavener, but it is a strong one. By that, I mean it reaches its peak leavening in 4 hours or so and is still at the same level after 12 hours of proofing—in marked contrast to the Russian culture described below. It has a distinctive flavor that I still haven't found the appropriate words to describe. I think it has a rather sour aftertaste. It is not a good culture for use in a bread machine.

When our son, Keith, a biochemist and avid sourdough baker, made a business trip to Finland, he was programmed to bring back a sourdough culture. He had to go to small villages and fight the language barrier, but he did come back with the culture and a book on Finnish breads.

THE RUSSIAN SOURDOUGH

This is the culture that will convince anyone that all sourdoughs are not the same. It is the fastest wild sourdough I have ever seen. If I use this culture on a daily basis, which I often do, it reaches its peak leavening rate in less than 1½ hours after I've taken it out of the refrigerator. And it leavens a loaf of bread in the same time or less. So why use anything else? Several reasons. It is intrinsically mild in flavor and sourness and it exhausts the nutrients in flour, becoming semidormant almost as fast as it reaches its peak leavening. For full flavor development it must proof overnight or 12 hours like any other culture. By the end of 12 hours, however, the wild yeast are sound asleep. If the loaves are formed at this point, they won't even start to rise for at least 1½ hours. This is no problem if your schedule permits, as mine usually does. I simply add 1 cup of flour to the dough after it has proofed about 10 hours. This gives the yeast a wakeup call and gets them working at full steam by the time the dough has been proofing for a total of 12 hours, which is when the loaves are formed. Because of its leavening speed, it is clearly the best culture for most bread machines. And a lot of bakers consider that mild flavor an asset. It will bake anything and, I confess, I use it more than any other culture.

Tanya Bevin, who is originally from Russia, contacted us in her attempt to bake breads as she remembered them. Her experience with commercial loaves was a culture shock, and she came to us desperately looking for an Old World starter that would enable her to bake bread as she remembered it. We gave her the Finnish culture. She lived in Seattle and worked as a tour guide to Russia. With her background in science and frequent trips to Russia, she seemed the ideal person to get a Russian culture. She brought back two from small villages north of Moscow. One is the most active sourdough culture we have seen.

Breads of North America

It is a mistake to overemphasize the importance of San Francisco and Yukon sour-doughs in the broad spectrum of North American breads. To be sure, those cultures are symbolic of the legends and present-day image of sourdough in this country. But the gold rush in California reached its zenith in 1849 and the Yukon strikes occurred some fifty years later. It is easy to forget that when the Pilgrims landed in 1620 they brought their sourdoughs with them. In the ensuing years of exploration, those cultures spread across the continent and made our bread for almost 230 years before gold was discovered in the West. That heritage of sourdough has left priceless sourdough cultures from Maine to New Mexico, from Florida to Alaska. And in spite of the convenience of commercial yeast, thousands of bread addicts and experts still choose the product made with sourdough. The sourdoughs of San Francisco and the Yukon are mere fledglings, but they fill a gap in our own short interval in time. Our Yukon culture passed from hand to hand directly from that source of unquestioned authenticity, a Yukon prospector. The San Francisco culture is from my grandmother in the Bay Area, who first acquired it more than fifty years previously. She fervently believed it dated to the gold rush of 1849.

THE YUKON SOURDOUGH

Our Yukon culture came to me by way of a medical school classmate, who ended up in Saudi Arabia practicing radiology in the same hospital in which I was a pathologist. We hadn't seen each other in twenty years, but it didn't take long for us to discover our mutual weakness—sourdough. I had my San Francisco culture with me, and he convinced his physician father to dry the Yukon culture and send us a few crumbs in a letter. The comparison of those two cultures convinced us both they were worlds apart, and the experience convinced me to search the world for more cultures, perhaps even to find the one that was used in humankind's first bread. The Yukon is moderately fast to leaven but slow for most bread machines except on the dough cycle. It is also moderately sour with a "Yukon" flavor. I have a host of friends that swear it is the only culture for real sourdough flapjacks.

SAN FRANCISCO SOURDOUGH

Now those are the words that makes mouths water! I'm frequently asked if this culture contains the wild yeast and lactobacilli of "the" San Francisco sourdough. I have the training to evaluate the culture, but I left all my microbiology facilities behind when I left the pathology laboratory. Unfortunately, the identification procedures are complex and expensive to perform. One of these days I may yet convince one of my former colleagues to tackle this awesome task. Considering the source, it likely contains the organisms of the San Francisco culture. However, based on the bread it produces, I believe it is a better culture. It leavens at a moderate rate and is moderately sour with a delicious flavor. It is not the best culture to use in a bread machine, but works with any bread made by hand.

Ordering Information

The cultures are $10.50 each, including shipping in the United States and Canada and (US) $13.00 in all other countries. (Prices may change.)

- To order a brochure: (800) 888-9567

- To place an order with Visa or Mastercard:
     208-382-3129 (fax)
     http://www.cyberhighway.net/~sourdo/

- To order with check or credit card, mail to:
     Sourdoughs International
     P.O. Box 670
     Cascade, ID 83611

SELECTED SOURCES

"After 4500 Years Rediscovering Egypt's Bread Baking Technology." *National Geographic* 187 (1995): 32–35.

El-Gendy, S. M. "Fermented Foods of Egypt and the Middle East." *Journal of Food Protection* 46 (1983): 358.

Gilliland, S. E. *Bacterial Starter Cultures for Foods*. (Boca Raton, FL: CRC Press, 1985).

Kline, Leo, and T. F. Sugihara. "Microorganisms of the San Francisco Sour Dough Bread Process. II. Isolation and Characterization of Undescribed Bacterial Species Responsible for the Souring Activity." *Applied Microbiology* 21 (1971): 459–465.

Mukherfee, S. K., et al. "Role of Leuconostoc mesenteroides in Leavening the Batter of Idli, a Fermented Food of India." *Applied Microbiology* 13 (1965): 227.

Ng, Henry. "Growth Requirements of San Francisco Sour Dough Yeasts and Baker's Yeast." *Applied and Environmental Microbiology* 31 (1976): 395–398.

Ortiz, Joe. *The Village Baker*. (Berkeley, CA: Ten Speed Press, 1993).

Spicher, G. "The Stimulators in Sourdough Fermentations." *Brot Gebaeck* 14 (1961): 27–32.

Sugihara, T. F., Leo Kline, and M. W. Miller. "Microorganisms of the San Francisco Sour Dough Bread Process. I. Yeasts Responsible for the Leavening Action." *Applied Microbiology*, 21 (1971): 456–458.

Zorzanello, D., and T. F. Sugihara. "The Technology of Pandoro Production." *Baker's Digest* 56 (1982): 12.

ED WOOD is a biologist and physician who studies living organisms and vital processes. Growing up in a conservation family imbued him with a love for wildlife, which led to a degree in fish and game management at Oregon State University. He pursued a Ph.D. at Cornell, where he studied under Dr. Clive McCay, one of the foremost pioneers in nutrition research in the United States, and Dr. Peter Olafson, an equal authority in animal pathology. From Cornell, Dr. Wood joined the U.S. Fish and Wildlife Service, where he did basic research on the pathology of trout and salmon. The challenging field of pathology drew him to the University of Washington and a degree of Doctor of Medicine, followed by a residency in human pathology. Along the way he served as a consultant for studies on diseases of the Olympia oyster and of cancer in trout. When *Apollo 11* returned from the moon, Dr. Wood was on the team at NASA's Lunar Receiving Laboratory to ensure that no lethal organisms from space would contaminate the earth. During all of this time a particular class

of truly unique organisms captured his imagination, the organisms of sourdough that produced man's bread for five thousand years.

In 1983 Dr. Wood became chairman of pathology at a new hospital for the Saudi Arabian National Guard at Riyadh, Saudi Arabia. Knowing that the Middle East was the historic birthplace of bread, he began a quest for sourdough cultures passed down through generations of bakers from the beginning of civilization. His adventures, ranging from the humorous to the serious, produced a collection of sourdoughs from around the world, some dating back to antiquity.

When he returned to the United States, he brought those cultures with him, along with all of the sourdough recipes he had encountered. Four years and hundreds of baking experiments later, he produced the first edition of *World Sourdoughs from Antiquity*, the first book on the science and art of sourdough. Today, he supplies wild sourdough cultures for avid bakers around the world, and says he is the only rancher to raise wild yeast and lactobacilli instead of livestock.

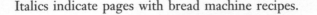

INDEX

Italics indicate pages with bread machine recipes.